KESWICK CHARACTERS
VOLUME ONE

Essays by
Margaret Armstrong
Jamie Barnes
Mary E Burkett, O.B.E.
Tony Greenbank
Alan Hankinson
Alan Smith
Brian Wilkinson

Edited by
Elizabeth Foot and Patricia Howell

Bookcase

GEORGE BOTT
A Dedication

'Keswick Characters' is dedicated to George Bott who, had he been alive, would no doubt have participated in this celebration of personalities who have enriched Keswick's life over many years.

George was an 'offcomer' who achieved fame as a local historian, scholar, raconteur and author who assiduously collected and filed newspaper cuttings and magazine articles concerning people associated with Keswick. His collection is now in the care of Keswick Historical Society (of which George was a founder member and president) and will be an invaluable resource for local historians in the future.

George's definitive history of Keswick 'Keswick, the Story of a Lake District Town' first published in 1994 includes references to many of the characters featured in this volume.

Members of Keswick Historical Society and Friends of Keswick Museum & Art Gallery wish to show by this dedication their appreciation of the efforts made by George to make our local history live for present and future generations to enjoy.

Keswick Characters: Volume One
Copyright Keswick Historical Society and Friends of Keswick Museum & Art Gallery and individual contributors, 2006
ISBN 190414716x
First Edition 2006
Published by Bookcase, 19 Castle Street, Carlisle, CA3 8SY
01228 544560   www.bookscumbria.com

Foreword

There's a well known description of Keswick which first appeared some 200 years ago in a guide book and is often quoted to either amuse or tease Keswickians today: 'The full perfection of Keswick consists of three circumstances - beauty, horror and immensity united.'

It's the use of the horror which intrigues. Could there have been tourists with their pasty thighs and garish cagoules walking six abreast down Main Street on a Bank Holiday two hundred years ago? Not quite. By 'horror' the guide book writer meant frightening crags, scary mountains, awesome ravines. Those three elements, all of which refer to landscape, are still true and perfect today, but the guide-book writer should have mentioned a fourth circumstance which Keswick has always been famous for – characters.

This first volume of Keswick Characters covers 400 years, and describes ten different characters. They range from a hermit to a historian, a clockmaker to a cleric. Some are nationally known, such as Canon Rawnsley, joint creator of the National Trust, or were nationally eminent, such as Sir John Bankes, Attorney General. Some are purely of Lakeland or local interest, like the dialect poet John Richardson. Some were pretty eccentric, not to say bizarre, known locally in their day but deserving of national attention and interest as Great British Characters, not just Keswick Characters. They include George Smith, the Skiddaw Hermit, and Joseph Richardson, creator of the Musical Stones, still to be seen, and heard, in Keswick Museum today, which once went of a tour of Europe and were played at Buckingham Palace.

The project is a collaboration between Friends of Keswick Museum – which of course we all should be, as it is such a marvellous institution – and Keswick Historical Society. Proceeds will go to towards supporting the Museum, which was first opened in 1898. It's still a Victorian gem, full of quirky collections. In 2003 it nearly closed for good, but was saved by the Friends and other volunteers.

Hurrah for that! And for all Keswick Characters. In the past, present and still to be . .

Hunter Davies
Loweswater, April 2006

The Contributors

Margaret Armstrong is a retired schoolteacher. She was secretary of the Keswick Historical Society for 16 years until 2001 and then became its president. She has written three books on local history.

Jamie Barnes is the Education and Exhibitions Officer at Keswick Museum and Art Gallery. Jamie has seven years experience of working in museums and galleries throughout the region. He can also play the ukulele, though others wish he wouldn't!

Mary E. Burkett, O.B.E. was Director of Abbott Hall Art Gallery and Museum in Kendal for many years. She has done much to support art and artists throughout Cumbria.

Elizabeth Foot used to work for the Open University in Manchester. After camping annually in Stonethwaite, Borrowdale, for over 30 years, she now lives in Braithwaite.

Tony Greenbank lives in Ambleside. He is a freelance journalist and writes the Lake District instalments of the 'Country Diary' in the Guardian, following in the footsteps of Harry Griffin.

Alan Hankinson is a former freelance journalist and author, now living in retirement in France and Keswick. His books include *A Century on the Crags*, the story of rock climbing in the English Lake District and the prize-winning *Coleridge Walks the Fells*.

Patricia Howell retired to Keswick in 2003 after a career in adult education. As a child she disliked history but has now discovered the pleasure derived from delving into the past.

Alan Smith is retired from an academic career and lives in Keswick. He has had a lifelong interest in Lakeland and has written widely on various aspects of its geology and landscape.

Brian Wilkinson is a retired primary school headteacher with a fascination for everything Cumbrian and especially its dialect and history. Born in Derbyshire, he came to Keswick with his family in 1966.

Contents

Dedication to George Bott
Foreword by Hunter Davies
1 Sir John Bankes 1589-1644
2 Jonathan Otley 1766-1856
3 Joseph Richardson & Sons 1790-1855
4 Henry Cowper Marshall 1808-1884
5 John Richardson 1817-1886
6 George Smith - the Skiddaw Hermit 1825-1876
7 James Clifton Ward 1843-1880
8 Hardwicke Drummond Rawnsley 1851-1920
9 Tom Wilson 1887-1961
10 Ray McHaffie 1936-2005

Acknowledgement.

The Production Team for 'Keswick Characters' wishes to acknowledge that an important stimulus for their venture was the booklet 'Caldbeck Characters' published by the Caldbeck & District Local History Society in 1995.

SIR JOHN BANKES, D.C.L. (1598 - 1644)
A man of great abilities and unblemished integrity

Brian Wilkinson

The year is 1589 and Queen Elizabeth is on the throne of England. Keswick, a town of not more than one thousand souls, is merely a line of dwellings fronting Main Street, in effect the Market Place. The Moot Hall, serving as a courthouse and jail, dominates the town.

In a lonely farmhouse, looking across Derwentwater, Elizabeth Bankes, a statesman farmer's wife, is giving birth to her first-born. Her son John was to become one of the most important men in England, admired for his forthrightness and honesty by both friend and foe and to have the ear of kings and princes.

John Bankes was said to have been born at Castlerigg, Rakefoot, near

Above: Portrait of Sir John Bankes.

Keswick in May or August of 1589 to an old Cumberland farming family. The precise location of the birthplace cannot be stated with certainty, but it is quite possibly the sixteenth/seventeenth-century house which is now known as Castlerigg Hall, the centre of an award-winning camping and caravanning site. John's father and grandfather were both named John and his mother was Elizabeth Hassell (Jane Malton, according to the Dictionary of National Biography). In 1602 the family home was a manor house in Main Street, opposite the Moot Hall, where, according to one account, John senior was in business as a merchant. An oak-panelled wall and a remnant of a moulded plaster ceiling remain from former days and parts of the original ceiling, with the date 1602, are displayed in the Keswick Museum. The stone plaque on the house (Bankes mis-spelt) reads:

Traditionally the home of Sir John Banks P.C. (1589 - 1644).
Lord Chief Justice of Common Pleas 1641

John Bankes attended the Free Grammar School by the church of St Kentigern at Crosthwaite. There he was taught mathematics, Greek and Latin and from there, in 1604, at the age of fifteen years, he entered Queen's College, Oxford.

John left Keswick and travelled the long road to join other young men from Cumberland and Westmorland at Queen's. He travelled on horseback on the rough highways, but with companions, as a lonely traveller could be accosted by robbers. Travel by road then was dirty, slow and dangerous. A hired horse could only cover some thirty miles a day and John's journey to Oxford would have taken several weeks.

Queen's College was founded in 1341 by Robert de Eglesfield (Eaglesfield is a village near Cockermouth), a chaplain to the household of Queen Philippa of Hainault, wife of Edward III. The founder named the college Queen's in her honour. At first, membership of the college was open to all comers, but with a preference for students from Cumberland and Westmorland. The college coat of arms, three eagles, is derived from the name of the founding chaplain.

John left Queen's College in 1607 without taking a degree, and entered Gray's Inn in London, where he distinguished himself by his application to the study of law.

According to Thomas Fuller's Worthies, 'Sir John Bankes was born at Keswick, of honest parents, who perceiving him judicious and

Lady Mary Banks

industrious, bestowed good breeding on him in Gray's Inn, in the hope he should attain to preferment; wherein they were not deceived.' At Gray's Inn 'he distinguished himself by his uncommon application to the study of the law, in which he acquired great eminence and reputation.'

John was called to the Bar in 1614 and in 1624 became Member of Parliament for Wootton Bassett in Wiltshire (a rotten borough with a population of less than two thousand and an electorate of only twenty) and then, in 1626 and 1628 was elected. member for Morpeth in Northumberland, almost certainly thanks to the influence of Lord William Howard of Naworth (Brampton, Cumberland) for whom he had acted professionally on several occasions.

After the dissolution of the monasteries Borrowdale had come into the possession of King Henry VIII. Eventually, by 1516, all the farms in the valley were bought by the tenants 'except all those wad holes (graphite) commonly called black cawke, within the Commons of Seatoller'. In March 1622 John Bankes bought a half-share in the mines from John

Kingston Lacy Hall

Lamplugh. Thus the wealth of the Bankes family was assured, and the mines 'were wrought with success'.

John Bankes married Mary Hawtrey of Ruislip, then a village outside London, in 1618. They had fourteen children, Alice, Mary, John, Elizabeth, Joan, Ralph, Jane, Jerome, Edward, Charles, Arabella, William, Bridget and Ann.

John achieved great eminence and reputation in law and, in 1631, was appointed Attorney-General to the infant Prince Charles and in 1634 Attorney-General to the King himself. He was knighted in June 1631.

Sir John Bankes is the only native-born Keswickian who has achieved both national fame and a high rank in the judiciary. It was said that 'He exceeds Bacon in eloquence (Sir Francis Bacon), Chancellor Ellesmere in judgement (Sir John Davies) and William Noy in law' (a noted English jurist). Charles I, though critical of Sir John's independent judgement, which amounted to stubbornness, 'never lost his affection for his Attorney-General' (Viola Bankes).

Sir John's legal reputation and family wealth provided him with the means to buy Corfe Castle on the Isle of Purbeck in Dorset from Lady

Elizabeth Coke in 1635. By 1636 he had completed the purchase of the Kingston Lacy estate, also in Dorset.

Corfe Castle lies between Wareham and Swanage in Dorset on the Isle of Purbeck. The castle of today is what remains of an eleventh-century rebuilding of a ninth-century wooden structure.

In the thirteenth century King John improved the defences and built a hall and chapel. Henry III built more walls, a tower and a gatehouse. In 1572 Queen Elizabeth sold the castle to Sir Christopher Halton, her dancing master and supposed suitor, and in 1635 the castle was sold to Sir John Bankes. For Sir John, Corfe Castle was more of a second or holiday home rather than a primary residence, and he never had the pleasure of living there as a permanent home. Lady Bankes lived in London, spending the summer months at Corfe Castle.

Kingston Lacy was initially established as the centre of a large royal estate in Anglo-Saxon times. In 1170 it was known as 'Kingestune' - the addition 'Lacy' came from medieval tenants, the De Lacys of Lincoln. Sir John never lived on the estate.

In 1640 (1641 in some accounts) Sir John was made Lord Chief Justice of the Common Pleas, a judicial office no longer existing. Prior to 1880, the appointment was one of the highest offices in England, second only to that of the Lord Chancellor.

Sir John, an avowed Royalist, remained in Westminster when the King left London for the north at the outbreak of the Civil War in 1642, but soon obeyed the royal summons to join the court in York. In June of 1642 he had been appointed a Privy Councillor and awarded the honorary degree of Doctor of Civil Law of Oxford on 20th December 1642.

He offended the King by not opposing the militia bill and was not given preferment when the position of Lord Chancellor became vacant. But, because of the respect in which he was held, he came to assume the role of mediator between King and Parliament.

The civil war depleted Sir John's finances and devastated the home he had created at Corfe Castle. He had garrisoned the Castle and left his wife to defend it whilst he went about the King's business and his legal responsibilities. 'Brave Dame Mary' as she became known, staunchly defended the castle.

By 1643 the Parliamentarians had occupied most of Dorset and Sir John was named as a traitor by Parliament. He remained in London whilst

Dame Mary was in charge of Corfe Castle. It was a tradition that the retainers and villagers would gather at the Castle on May Day for a deer hunt. This was seen as an opportunity for the local Parliamentary commander, Sir Walter Earl, to seize the castle whilst Sir John was attending to his legal duties in Salisbury. However, Lady Bankes cancelled the hunt that year. Sir Walter then sent a party of sailors from Poole to commandeer four cannon from the Castle with the intention of weakening the defences. Lady Bankes ordered a cannon to be fired as a warning, and the party dispersed. The cat and mouse game continued, with the Earl making it an offence to supply the Castle with supplies. Lady Bankes then allowed the four cannon to be removed, to buy time to prepare for the ensuing siege.

The Castle survived a six-week siege in the summer of 1643 when one hundred and fifty men came from Portsmouth with siege ladders to scale the walls. A prize of £20 was offered to the first man to scale the walls, worth £2000 today. Despite the bribe, the men were reluctant to attempt the climb and the Earl resorted to providing them with alcohol to give them Dutch courage. One hundred men were killed as they attempted to scale the walls, bombarded by rocks and hot cinders thrown by Lady Bankes's defenders - of whom only two were killed. With several local towns falling to the Royalists, the Earl's men fled, leaving their arms and provisions to be captured by Lady Bankes' retainers.

After a brief period of peace at Corfe Castle, Sir John returned to Oxford to the exiled court. There he died (one account gives the cause of death as 'the plague') aged 55 years, on 28th December 1644, tended by his two elder daughters, Lady Borlase (Alice) and Lady Jenkinson (Mary). Sir John was buried in Christ Church Cathedral, Oxford. The monument to his memory, in translation from the Latin, reads:

In this place, to the hope of
Years to come, lies buried
John Bankes
Who, in Queen's College
Was a pupil
A Knight, honoured in the most
distinguished manner
Attorney - General
Chief Justice of the Common Pleas

Corfe Castle

*Adviser to King Charles in the Privy Council
Particularly outstanding in his
Experience, his honesty and his good faith
He died on 28th December,
In the year of Our Lord 1644
Aged 55 years.*

In 1646 Colonel Bingham, the Governor of Poole, subjected the Castle to another siege with five hundred men. The Roundheads took the Castle by force on 27th February. The second siege of Corfe Castle lasted for forty-eight days and was only ended by the treachery of a member of the garrison who admitted Parliamentary troops into the Castle disguised as royalist reinforcements. Lady Bankes, 'Brave Dame Mary', was forced to agree a truce.

In March, Corfe Castle was 'slighted' (reduced to ruins) by Parliamentary gunpowder.

Dame Mary returned to her family home in Ruislip. In a gesture of defiance, she is said to have dropped her jewellery down the castle well - a treasure that has never been recovered. That act would be in character. Colonel Bingham, 'an honourable Dorset man', allowed her to leave with the keys of the Castle as a tribute to her courage. The keys still hang over the chimneypiece in the library of Kingston Lacy House. Lady Bankes survived her husband for another seventeen years and died on 11th April 1661 at Damory Court, Blandford.

On the south wall of the chancel of St Martin's Church, Ruislip, is her monument:

To the memory of LADY MARY BANKES, the only daughter of Ralph Hawtery, of Riselip, in the County of Middlesex, Esq.,
the wife and widow of the Honourable Sir John Bankes, Knight, late Lord Chief Justice of His Majesty's Court of Common Pleas, and of the Privy Council of His Majesty King Charles I of blessed memory, who having had the honour to have borne with a constancy and courage above her sex a noble proportion of the late calamities, and the restitution of the government with great peace of mind laid down her most desired life the 11th day of April 1661.
Sir Ralph Banckes her son and heir hath dedicated this.
She had four sons: 1.Sir Ralph; 2. Jerome; 3. Charles; 4. William (since dead without issue), and six daughters.

Dame Mary and her children had paid to regain the property confiscated by Parliament and the family was left in peace during the Commonwealth. In 1656 the first son of Sir John and Lady Mary, John, died unmarried at the age of thirty years and the second son, Ralph (1631?-1677) succeeded to the title. He became a lawyer, training at Gray's Inn, as his father had done and a Member of Parliament for Corfe Castle in Cromwell's Parliament, another rotten borough.

After Charles II came to the throne in 1660 the Bankes's family properties were restored. The family decided to concentrate their efforts on building a new house at the other estate in Dorset, Kingston Lacy.

Ralph was knighted by King Charles II and made a Privy Councillor in recognition of the part played by his family's support for the monarchy. In 1661 he married an heiress, Mary Brune, daughter of an old Dorset family - with an income of £1200 a year, a substantial amount at that time. Two years later they began the building of their family seat, Kingston Lacy Hall.

In 1853, when John William Bankes M.P. was the head of the family, a contract was signed in Paris for three monumental bronze statues to be placed on the staircase at Kingston Lacy at a cost of £2500. John Bankes wrote from Venice, 'Where will there be in any private home in England a family monument of such magnificence ?' Sadly, he died in 1855 without seeing the statues in place.

The bronzes, life-sized and sculpted by Carlo Marochetti, are of Sir John Bankes, Lady Mary and Charles I. The statue of Lady Mary has her holding a sword and the keys to Corfe Castle. Keswick's memorial to Sir John pales in comparison.

In 1981 both Corfe Castle and Kingston Lacy House, 'gradually subsiding into tranquil decay', were bequeathed by Ralph Bankes (1902 - 1981) to the National Trust and opened to the public in 1986 after extensive restoration.

The National Trust house stewards at Kingston Lacy pause with their conducted parties on the staircase, where the story of Sir John and Dame Mary is told, with reference to the humble beginnings of the family in Keswick and one source of their wealth, the graphite mines of Seathwaite, Borrowdale.

It is not known if Sir John and his wife ever visited Keswick together, but in his will, dated 1642, Sir John remembered his birthplace with a bequest to benefit the poor of his native town by the establishment of a poorhouse, sited where the present Post Office building stands at the Lower Market Place. In his will Sir John left £200 for the building of the poorhouse and £30 per annum for three years 'to raise a stock of wool, flax, hemp, thread, iron and other necessary wear and stuff to set the poor to work who were born in the Parish of Crosthwaite''. The plaque on the building reads:

This building stands on the site of the 'Workhouse' founded
by Sir John Bankes
who was born in this town in 1589, became Chief Justice of the
Common Pleas
and died in Oxford in 1644.
His love for his native place and his wise and
generous sympathy for the poor and needy are shown
by the endowment which happily still endures
and is known as 'Sir John Bankes Charity'

Inmates of the workhouse were to include children whose parents were unable to maintain them, orphans and widows, the ageing poor and indigent paupers. Profits from the sale of cloth and linen made by the inmates were to be directed to helping the halt and lame, the blind and the incapacitated, and to organising apprenticeships.

It appears that Sir John's insistence on gainful employment was ignored and what had been intended as a workhouse had declined into a comparatively comfortable parish poorhouse. Its popularity grew so much that 'the Great House', as it was called, had at times up to eighty inmates, among them whole families.

The Poor Law of 1834 put a stop to such intensive use. The influence of Robert Southey with the Charity Commissioners ensured its continuance but the number of residents was reduced to eighteen poor and aged persons.

The 1862 Enquiry by the Charity Commissioners into Keswick's sixteen local charities, one of which was Bankes's, ordered that the poorhouse should be closed and the funds used to provide relief for selected impoverished Keswickians who would, as a result, be able to maintain their own homes rather than spend their declining years in the nearest workhouse at Cockermouth.

A bust of Sir John Bankes is situated in the Upper Fitz Park, Keswick. The inscription reads:

In honour of Sir John Bankes, a native and benefactor of this town.
Born at Castlerigg 1589.
Attorney General 1634. Lord Chief Justice of Common Pleas 1640.
Died at Oxford 1644

The story of the erection of the bust is an intriguing one. It was decided in 1889 that there should be a permanent and appropriate recognition of the great man in Keswick. H D Rawnsley, then vicar of Crosthwaite, was approached with the suggestion that a bronze statue, seated and life-sized, should be placed in the Lower Market Place near the site of the Sir John Bankes's Poorhouse, or 'some emblem of art and commerce, incorporating a medallion with portraits of Sir John and 'Brave Mary' be placed in the vicinity'.

But there was a movement in the town to displace H. D. Rawnsley as chairman of the organising committee, with the result that the whole committee resigned and the project failed. Perhaps it was thought that Rawnsley, vicar of Crosthwaite for only six years, was getting above himself! Eliza Lynn Linton, born at Crosthwaite Vicarage in 1822, Keswick's only indigenous author and the first professional woman journalist, wrote an eloquent article in The Times supporting the proposal, but to no avail.

Eliza had no illusions about her native town and the people there. She wrote later, 'I see the dear vale keeps up its fighting blood. What a beloved set of fractious figures they are! Can they not possibly agree on anything under the sun ? I wonder they all accept the arithmetic of the schoolmaster . . . that some of them do not take off their coats for two and two making five!'

Another attempt to erect a memorial took place in 1893, with the suggestion that a brass mural in Crosthwaite Church, a cottage hospital or a scholarship for boys would be acceptable, but this plan too ended in naught and it was not until 1903, more than two hundred and fifty years after his death, that action was taken which culminated in a memorial to Sir John. A committee was formed to raise funds for a bronze bust - 'a too-long delayed memorial to a great Englishman' - but not in the Lower Market Place.

The proposition was to have this bust placed in the Upper Fitz Park. Not all the Fitz Park Trustees were in favour of this either. But, by April 1904 the memorial was in place, a bronze cast from a model by Adolphus Rost set on a plinth of Aberdeen granite. In itself, it is a handsome tribute to a great man.

There the bust stands, hidden under a tree and unnoticed by many of the visitors and local people who visit the Park. Occasionally, when the Keswick Street Theatre Players pass that way with their Town Trail, a local actor appears in costume from behind the statue to the delight and amazement of the audience. On Tuesday evenings in June and July Sir John comes alive!

According to St. Matthew's gospel, 'A prophet is not without honour, save in his own country, and in his own house'. Sir John's rise from a yeoman farmer's family to the highest offices of state, and his remarkable character, surely deserve better recognition from his native town.

Further reading:
Viola Bankes: *A Dorset Heritage, the Story of Kingston Lacy*, 1953
George Bott: *Keswick - The Story of a Lake District Town,* 1994
Thomas Fuller: *A History of the Worthies of England*, 1662
Anthony Mitchell: *Kingston Lacy, The National Trust*, 1994

JONATHAN OTLEY (1766 - 1856)
Clockmaker, Geologist and Guide-Book Writer

Alan Smith

There have been several accounts written about the life and work of Jonathan Otley, describing him variously as 'geologist', 'clockmaker', 'guide-book writer', 'meteorologist', 'map maker', 'mountain guide', 'scientist', or 'natural historian'. 'Pioneering geologist' may be a better description, for undoubtedly his work in this field was seminal. 'Local worthy' also comes to mind as his contribution to Keswick life in many spheres was outstanding and lasting. In his day his name frequently became prefixed with 'old' as he lived and worked in the town until he was over 90, with his workshop and cottage known by every Keswickian as

Above: Jonathan Otley artist and date unknown. (Keswick Museum and Art Gallery)

Drawing of Scroggs, possibly by T. Binns, Halifax, circa 1840.

'Jonathan Otley's up t'steps'. Outside Cumbria he should be better known for he corresponded with many famous names and his work was highly regarded by some influential people, but at heart he was a reserved, modest Cumbrian who scarcely travelled far from his roots, but left an outstanding local legacy.

Jonathan Otley was born on January 19th 1766 at a house called Scroggs (formerly called Nook House) at Loughrigg, near Grasmere in south Lakeland. He had an older brother Edward and a sister Jane, two years his junior. Otleys had lived in the parish for over two hundred and fifty years. However, his mother came originally from Satterthwaite near Coniston. Although he was a child from a humble family he was encouraged to study and he attended a dame school at Lane Ends, Elterwater and schools in Langdale and Ambleside. His father taught him Latin and mathematics. Up to the age of 25 he worked with his father making wooden sieves and baskets, but he also developed the skills of watch and clock repairing. He was extremely inquisitive, taking watches and clocks apart to find out how they worked, and began to repair timepieces for neighbours and passing pack pony drivers. He also became very skilful in engraving on copper plates, seals and coins.

He was of a shy and retiring disposition and had a slight speech impediment. As a young man he courted and fell in love with a local girl,

Ann Youdale. He engraved both his and Ann's name together on a silver coin, but in spite of this, she fell for the local blacksmith, a Mr Bowness, leaving someone to comment much later that 'clearly the smith knew when to strike when the iron was hot'. Shortly after this, Jonathan left the family home in Loughrigg and moved on his own to Keswick. Whether this was the result of his unrequited love, or more likely the need to find work and establish himself is unknown.

He first lodged in Keswick with a Mr Younghusband at Brow Top, a farmstead on the Ambleside Road. He established a small shop and workshop there, repairing clocks and watches. He had a small window facing the road where he could display his wares and a sign announcing 'Jonathan Otley, Clockmaker and Engraver'. He paid what was considered very handsome for his board at the time - one shilling a day, all found. He once remarked to his host that the Sundays should be thrown in, but was given the curt reply 'No, no man; we boil the pot on Sundays'. Five and half years later he moved into the town centre, into a cottage/workshop in King's Head Court which became known as 'Jonathan Otley's up t'steps' where he stayed for almost all of his long life. Again Otley was lodging; here he paid 6s per week for his board to a Mr John Robson. His workshop was the adjoining room which he paid a further 1s per week to a Mr George Rookin. The doorway of this cottage still exists with the stone steps leading up to it. Alongside on the wall is a plaque to his memory. The inside of the cottage has long since been

Otley's cottage up t'steps Kings Head Court.

converted and is now one of Keswick's numerous outdoor clothing stores, but from the outside it is not hard to visualise Otley working and living here in this narrow yard at the very heart of the town. During the summer months today Otley's life in Keswick is often remembered here with a re-enactment of his appearance at the top of the steps by a member of the Keswick Street Theatre Group suitably attired in his long frock coat.

Using King's Head Court as his base Otley came to know the Lakeland fells and dales like the back of his own hand. From his writings and correspondence, much of which is preserved, it is clear he walked the ground and made meticulous lists and notes of his observations. His particular interest was in the rocks and the Lakeland landscape, but he also became an authority on the natural history, Lakeland topography and a recorder of weather and meteorology. He produced some important early maps of Lakeland and perhaps received most popular recognition as a local guide and more particularly as a guide-book writer. For a time he developed a sideline in land surveying. Much common land was being enclosed at the time and his meticulous nature for recording and his ability to make simple surveying instruments enabled him to find work in this area. All of these activities produced income and it would be interesting to know the extent to which he relied upon his watch and clock repairing for a livelihood, which seems to be the reason why he came to Keswick in the first place. The plaque on the wall of his cottage describes him as geologist and clockmaker. Penfold in his 'The Clockmakers of Cumberland' (1977) however, states that 'there is no evidence he ever made a clock'. Cleaning and fettling watches and clocks were probably his limits. In 1800, a lever watch, then a novelty, was presented to him but it was beyond his skill. We know he spent some time in 1841 repairing the clock at Crosthwaite Church. He made regular summertime holiday visits back to his birthplace at Loughrigg and it is recorded that he always had a steady stream of watches and clocks from the locals to attend to when he was there.

Otley's work as a geologist never gained the acclamation it deserved in his lifetime. Outside Cumbria he was not well known and as he rarely ventured far from his base in Keswick it was left to others to make his ideas and observations known on the national scene. He corresponded with many of the eminent scientists of his day and unselfishly fed many of them with information from his observations. In his time, the towering figure in British geology was another Cumbrian (from Dent), Adam Sedgwick. From his commanding position as the first Professor of Geology at Cambridge he is the one who is usually credited with the earliest exposition of the major geological features of the Lake District. It is arguable that Sedgwick could not have made such early progress without the help of Otley.

Otley first published his essay on the geological structure of the Lake District in the Philosophical Magazine in 1820 and also in the first volume of a short-lived local journal, the Lonsdale Magazine, in the same year. However, it was in his guide books that the material was most read and progressively developed in the various editions up to the middle of the century. In the first paragraph of the 1830 edition of the Guide he remarks: 'At the time this essay was first published in 1820 the structure of the mountainous district of Cumberland, Westmorland and Lancashire was but little understood; scientific travellers had contented themselves with procuring specimens of the different rocks, without taking time to become acquainted with their relative position.' He goes on to point out that 'The greater part of the central region of the Lake mountains is occupied by three distinct groups of stratified rocks of a slaty texture.' These he called the Clayslate, Greenstone and the Greywacke - remarkably perceptive descriptions of the three familiar group of rocks which we now know make up the centre of the Lake District and we now term the Skiddaw Group, the Borrowdale Volcanic Group and the Windermere Supergroup. Otley had clearly worked this out long before 1820.

In September 1823 he introduced Sedgwick to the rocks of the Skiddaw area in the first of their field excursions. It was not until 1831 that Sedgwick went into print with his ideas on the structure of the district. In his address to the Geological Society of London in that year he acknowledged that it was Otley who first recognised the three distinct groups of stratified rocks in the district. Later, in 1836, Sedgwick in a paper to the Geological Society entitled 'Introduction to the General Structure of the Cumbrian Mountains', after describing the various subdivisions of the altered slate around the Skiddaw Granite (the location of the pair's first excursion in 1823) goes on to say: 'We owe our first accurate knowledge of these subdivisions to Mr Jonathan Otley of Keswick, who not merely described them in general terms but gave their geographical distribution with a very near approach to accuracy.'

An examination of Otley's descriptions of the three great rock groups of the Lake District reveals not only his intimate knowledge and observations of the area but, more importantly, his insight into what these rocks were telling him of their history. The Clayslate (Skiddaw Group) he recognised as the oldest group and commented on its great structural complexity. He remarks on its variability, its weaknesses as a useful building material, its intrusion by complex dyke systems and its rich mineralogy. Equally his descriptions of the Greenstones (the volcanics) were remarkably accurate. Not only was he able to describe what he saw, he also seemed able to perceive which features did not quite fit into the general pattern of things and perhaps had special circumstances surrounding them. He clearly drew the distinctions between the lavas and what we now know are the pyroclastic materials (ashes) with a strong slaty structure. But, even more intuitively, his observations of the volcanics on Binsey and of the northern Caldbeck Fells were telling him there was something rather different here. Only relatively recently has it been demonstrated that they are in fact a chemically distinct group and the product of a separate early phase of volcanic activity. He knew of the red haematite breccias in the volcanic rocks of the Keswick area and carefully described the presence of garnets in the volcanic rocks - a puzzling geological problem that has tested the best geological brains ever since.

The Greywacke (Windermere Supergroup) of the southern Lakes he observed with equal insight. In his guide we read ... 'The Third Division - forming only inferior elevations - commences with a bed of dark blue or blackish transition limestone, containing here and there a few shells and madrepores, and alternating with a slaty rock of the same colour; the different layers of each being in some places several feet and in others only a few inches in thickness. This limestone crosses the River Duddon near Broughton; passing Broughton Mills it runs in a N.E. direction through Torver, by the foot of the Old Man Mountain, and appears near Low Yewdale. Here it makes a considerable slip to the eastward, after which it ranges past the Tarns upon the hills above Borwick Ground, and after stretching through Skelwith, it traverses the vales of Troutbeck, Kentmere and Longsleddal'. To have produced such an accurate description of what has since been known as the faulted outcrop of the Coniston Limestone not only illustrates pioneeringly perceptive geological mapping but immense physical effort tramping on foot over terrain which even today is not highly accessible nor hospitable. Bearing in mind this was a time long before the existence of accurate Ordnance Survey maps his achievements are all the more remarkable.

Of a more technical nature perhaps Otley's greatest geological achievement was his exposition of the relationship between bedding, cleavage and jointing in the Lake District rocks. Even today the fundamental differences between these properties and their structural implications are not always easy to grasp, and in many field situations in Lakeland they have to be established before the geological story can be revealed.

Many other examples of his field observations and early understanding of Lakeland rocks and landscapes exist. He clearly understood the zonation in the metamorphic rocks surrounding the Skiddaw Granite and introduced Sedgwick and others to that area. He delineated the Shap and Eskdale Granite intrusions and described the Armboth Fell Dyke. Surprisingly he seems to have had little interest in palaeontology, referring only fleetingly to fossil finds. He appears to have been rather unsure how to explain the existence of erratic boulders. His knowledge of the pattern of outcrops and of the topography was telling him that these stray boulders needed explaining. He describes and locates many examples and saw that some powerful erosive agent had carried them, often across the topography. Some, like the Bowder Stone in Borrowdale, he rightly saw as a product of rock fall. What he described as 'rounded and smoothed surfaces ... some striped and scored in a remarkable manner' in Borrowdale and Langdale also illustrates his uncertainty about landscape forming processes. His conclusion however that 'some, who have become converts to a recently promulgated theory will attribute those appearances to the agency of GLACIERS; but the action of WATER seems more intelligible to the mere English Geologist'.... leaves no doubt where he stood on this debate.

Otley led Sedgwick on a number of field excursions around the district, starting in the summer of 1823. This was the start of a long association between the two men. Correspondence between them for almost 30 years from 1827 to 1855 still exists. Sedgwick came regularly during the summer to see Otley and to walk the fells with him. In 1836 they climbed Helvellyn and Skiddaw. Otley also corresponded with John Dalton, another Cumbrian, G. B. Airey, the then Astronomer Royal, and

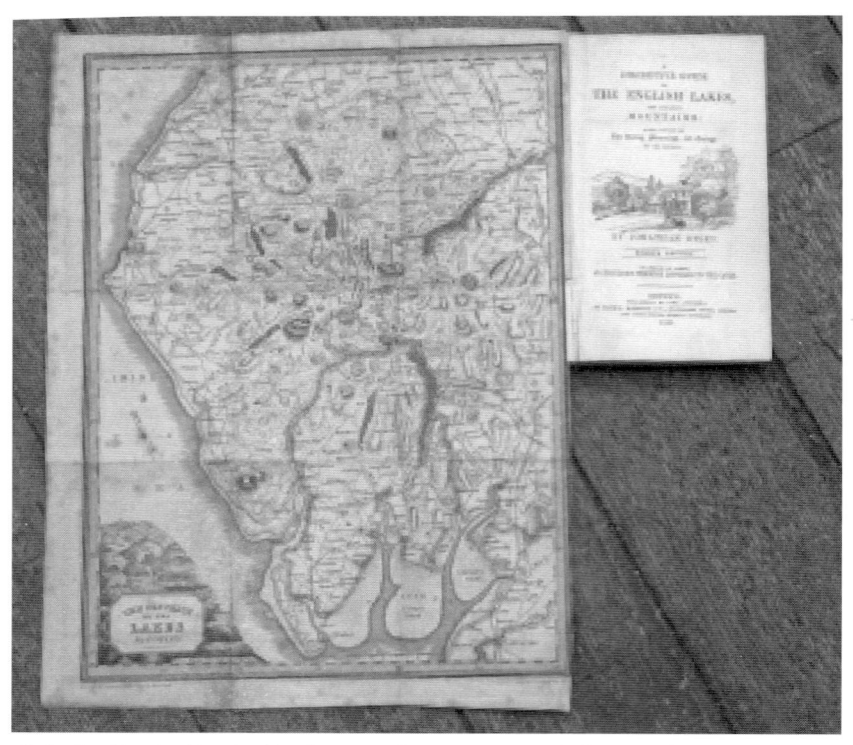

Otley's Guide Book, A Concise Description of the English Lakes and Adjacent Mountains (Eighth Edition 1849), showing the fold-out topographical map in the front of the guide with the title page..

the geologist Professor John Phillips, the Museum curator at York. Otley's early observations on bedding, cleavage and jointing in rocks were later defined more clearly by Phillips, but Otley was the instigator and saw the significance of these features. He also met William Smith, the so-called 'Father of English Geology' who in 1815 had astounded the scientific world by publishing the first geological map of England - in fact the first geological map in the world. His story has recently been told in the bestselling book by Simon Winchester 'The Map that Changed the World'. Smith came on his first visit to the Lakes in 1823 staying in Hesket Newmarket and Otley escorted him around the Skiddaw area, although their meeting was apparently not totally amicable. Smith was an irascible character, of very different temperament to Otley.

Otley initially gained public recognition through his topographical map of the Lake District which he produced in 1817 and had engraved and published the following year. It was chiefly sold folded for the pocket. It contained a remarkable amount of detail of the topography of the mountains and dales, and had drawings of the mountain outlines that were very accurate and lacking the exaggeration of many earlier attempts to portray the district. In 1823 he published the accompanying guide book:- *A concise description of the English Lakes and adjacent mountains*. This contained descriptions of the lakes and mountains, with 'stages' that the tourist should visit. Additionally he included a series of his essays on the district, notably the one on geology. It ran to 136 pages, was priced at 4s. 6d and sold 600 copies. Subsequent editions in 1825 and 1827 reconstructed and improved the map. The fourth edition in 1830 included eight of his own woodcuts and a new essay on the botany of the district. The fifth and sixth editions saw more woodcuts and new copper engravings. By 1849 with the eighth edition it was then 216 pages long, with 46 illustrations. In total 8450 copies of the guides were sold. All are now sought after in the second hand book trade and command high prices. The income from these must have been quite significant for Otley.

Apart from his guide-books he was not a particularly prolific writer but what he did produce was done with great care and was plainly to the point. His earliest work was a paper on the Black Lead Mine (plumbago) in Borrowdale, read before the Manchester Philosophical Society on December 27th 1816. (An interesting date - it would nice to know how and when Otley made this journey down to Manchester: perhaps a Christmas holiday wasn't important to him). It was a comprehensive account of what was then known about this unique deposit. In 1819 the same society published his paper on the Floating Island in Derwentwater - the first systematic account of this feature compiled from his very detailed field observations, done over many seasons. He was able to describe how the island occasionally rises from the bottom of the lake to the surface, and how it is related to periods of dry summer conditions between June and September. He saw it was related to decaying vegetation liberating gas, which gave buoyancy to the mat of vegetation. In a letter to John Dalton in September 1815 he refers to samples of the gas that Dalton had analysed for him, and of samples of the vegetative matter that he had systematically sampled from the surface, from varying depths within the island and from the water beneath. This was typical of the thoroughness of his observational work in the field. There was a second paper of further observations of the island in the same journal in 1831, illustrating his perseverance in continuously observing natural phenomena.

There remains an interesting, and as yet partly unanswered question, as whether Otley ever produced a geological map of the Lake District. It is hard to believe that someone with Otley's talents for map making and his knowledge of the regional geological pattern did not at least produce some drafts or sketches of a geological map. Otley and Sedgwick clearly exchanged topographical sketch maps. A letter from Otley to Sedgwick of January 30th 1828 refers to some errors Sedgwick had incorporated in a map of the Skiddaw area. More interestingly, Sedgwick in a letter to Otley dated February 14th 1847 writes: 'Do you wish to publish a geological map of your country, on a scale of your Lake map? If so, I would most willingly help you to the best of my power; and you might use my name in any way you thought fit. I think such a map, with a short explanatory sheet, might have a sale.' Sedgwick clearly seems to suggest Otley should commit his knowledge of the region on to a map. Otley replied to Sedgwick on February 24th 1847 saying that Mr Farey from the Black Lead mines in Borrowdale had also suggested that he (Otley) should consider putting his geological knowledge on to a map. Otley went on: 'I have tried a few, but could not entirely satisfy myself, and did not find it likely to be profitable. I sold to Dr Buckland and Mr Greenough each one, with a sheet taken out of the Guide, at 5s each.'. (Both Buckland and Greenough were eminent geologists of the time.) Whether he did any more or made further attempts is not known. Authentic records of these cannot be located. One of Otley's 1837 topographic maps, coloured geologically, is in the archive of the Geological Society of London, but who coloured it is not clear and whether it might have been either Buckland's or Greenough's, both prominent members of the Geological Society, remains a mystery.

Otley had a keen interest in meteorology and was an ardent recorder of weather conditions in Keswick. He maintained continuous observations between 1844 and 1855, particularly from his rain gauge which he had set up in Crow Park. Clifton Ward writing about Otley in 1877 describes a

Otley's Well, on the banks of the River Greta, close to the junction of Greta Street and the Penrith Road.
Below: Close up showing the inscription in the lintel above the arch.

manuscript book containing his observations all carefully written out and tabulated. He remarked further that he trusted Mr Crosthwaite (at the Museum) would incorporate these with his own observations at some future time. Sadly this didn't happen and the whereabouts of Otley's manuscript books of his observations seems to have been lost. He took temperatures at many places in the valleys and on the fells and kept constant records of the level of Derwentwater. At Friars Crag where there are numerous plaques and markers recording high and low lake levels he is reputed to have cut a notch

Jonathan Otley in later life (date unknown)

in the rock, which is still visible today, as his own datum line from which to make his observations. He also kept extensive botanical notes and apparently gathered roots and cuttings which he replanted in a series of local dells and beauty spots which he particularly admired. Otley also had a long fascination with springs and wells and was undoubtedly consulted on the problems of water supply in the town. He analysed the water quality of many local sources and was concerned about the purity of local supplies. A spring he was particularly fond of was 'the Fairy Keld' hidden in the woods at the foot of Walla Crag and another one on Barrow Common. In the preface to the eighth edition of his guide it is recorded that he constantly tried to keep these wells sweet and clear and went to the length of planting hyacinth bulbs, water cress, scurvy grass, veronica and forget-me-not around them. He had an involvement with a well at the end of Greta Street at its junction with the Penrith Road. At some stage this became known as Otley's Well. It had water of high purity and was used for special jobs, notably for washing fine fabrics and with additions for medicinal prescriptions. At some stage the well was protected and enhanced with some fine masonry and an inscription on the lintel above it. This is still there today. It is difficult to see from the main Penrith Road but from across the river in Fitz Park it stands out in the wall of the river bank. He was also an advocate in his day of a public piped water supply for the town from Brockley Beck (Gale) at Underskiddaw, which in his old age he saw completed.

During his long life Otley clearly became a well-known character in Keswick. He was a quiet, reserved, modest man who never married. It is clear from his correspondence and from contemporary accounts that he was renowned as a listener rather than a talker, a thinker who offered an opinion only when he had thought through and grasped the whole matter. He established himself as an authority on many aspects of Lakeland life and was consulted widely on the details of the local topography, the heights of the fells, lake levels, details of the mineral veins, the state of the wind, helm and bottom winds in the valleys. He seems to have been quite fond of society and especially of some of the ladies of his acquaintance. It is reported he 'would go to a picnic to have tea with a large party of friends and gaily bring the hostess to his arm into the ring where the cloth was spread on the green'. He knew many of the eminent Keswick personalities of his day. Peter Crosthwaite, the Museum keeper was a close friend and clearly lent Otley books. The poet Southey at Greta Hall also befriended Otley, and his extensive library was at Otley's disposal. Otley's letters also refer repeatedly to a Charles Wright who was a geological friend and local collector. For a time he had a local nickname 'Anthony Loajet' (an anagram of his name); who first used it is not known but Otley refers to it in some of his correspondence and clearly took it in good part. Sunday was Jonathan's day of rest. His pew at Crosthwaite Church was generally occupied by him. Perhaps as a sign of his modesty and shyness it was a single pew up against a pillar. His name appears in the vestry registers as a member of the bible class run by James Stanger, the restorer of Crosthwaite church.

Otley became progressively more infirm in later life. He found the stairs up to his cottage in King's Head Court more and more difficult to negotiate. He gave up the walk to Crow Park to tend his weather instruments and became less able to get out on to the fells. In his letters to Sedwick he frequently refers to his health and his longing to explore the countryside. He admitted to being lonely. In 1853 at the age of 87 he moved to a small cottage in St John's Street next to Miss Pettitt's Photographers Shop (now the hairdressers opposite the cinema). His niece Jane came to keep house for him. He was too old to carry on with his watch and clock repairing, or his surveying and engraving, so he decided to disperse all his instruments, tools and books by public auction. There were more than 300 lots and after paying off expenses he was left with £20. Some were bought by local enthusiasts and fortunately some eventually found their way into the present Keswick Museum. There is a good selection of his surveying instruments, tripods, his rain gauge from

Crow Park and some personal items like his spectacles. As his physical health deteriorated he nevertheless kept mentally very alert and some of his letters to Sedgwick and others when he was close to 90 demonstrate his ability to write in a firm hand and with a clear mind. Sedgwick came to see Otley on his deathbed, speechless and paralysed, days before he died aged 91 on December 7th 1856. He made his own will, disposing of some £3000, 'with all legacies to be paid within three months'.

The people of Keswick were saddened by his passing and came out in great numbers to his funeral. The shops in the town were closed as a mark of respect and a large procession of mourners singing hymns passed through the town on the way to Crosthwaite Church. His grave, now rather hidden with bushes, is on the north side of the graveyard close to the church.

If Otley is not remembered much nationally in geological circles, he has not been forgotten in Keswick. The plaque on his cottage was erected to mark the centenary of his death. Otley Well bears his name although hundreds of people pass it daily without realising it is there. More obvious is Otley Road, a narrow thoroughfare close to the town centre, which now, although it is mainly a car park, keeps the Otley name in the Keswick memory. The Museum collection of his tools and instruments keeps part of his story alive. We have a few portraits, but sadly many of his original notebooks, records and letters have disappeared. It was in his contribution to our early understanding of the geology of the Lake District, his map and guide books and his life as a nature lover and devoted man of Lakeland that he will be best remembered.

Further reading.
Otley's work is best appreciated by looking at his maps and guide books or by reading his own accounts of the black lead mines and the floating island on Derwentwater.
Accounts of his life and work include:
Tom Wilson: *Jonathan Otley, Keswick's Back-Room Boy, Keswick Reminder* 1955.
D.R. Leitch: *A Memoir of Jonathan Otley*, Keswick 1882.
B. Wilkinson: *Jonathan Otley, Clockmaker and Geologist 1766-1856* in Alan Sykes (Edit): *Persons and Places in Langdale History*, 2005.

For and evaluation of Otley as geologist and a full referencing of his writing see:

Alan Smith: *Jonathan Otley, 'Father of Lakeland Geology,* in *The Rock Men: Pioneers of Lakeland Geology, Cumberland Geological Society,* pp 2-9 *or* Alan Smith: *Jonathan Otley, a Pioneer of Lakeland Geology, Geology Today, vol. 16. No 1,* pp31-4.

For Otley's letters and correspondence see J.C. Ward*: Trans. Cumb. & West. Assoc. Adv. Lit & Sci. Pt 2. pp 125-69.* 1887.

JOSEPH RICHARDSON (1790 - 1855) & SONS
and the Famous Musical Stones of Skiddaw

Jamie Barnes

If you cross the threshold of the Keswick Museum and Art Gallery and look to your right you will see two curious musical instruments. They look like xylophones, but the notes are not made from metal or wood, but from a local stone. These two objects represent a fascinating 220 year-long story full of obsession, changing fortunes, glory and international fame. The story even continues today, with a new touring and performance schedule.

The first person to find music in the stones around Keswick was the incomparable Peter Crosthwaite. Born at Dale Head, Thirlmere in 1735, he joined the East India Company after a brief and unhappy venture into his family's woollen business. He became a naval commander, Master of the gunboat 'Otter', protecting the Company's ships against Malay pirates.

Joseph Richardson and Sons and the Rock Bell and Steel and Band, from an engraving on show at Keswick Museum and Art Gallery

Richardson's Original Rock, Bell and Steel Band

He returned to England in 1765 and undertook customs duties on the coast before returning to Keswick in 1779 and setting up a museum there in 1780.

Crosthwaite was an incredible eccentric, and a very keen inventor. His inventions included a fire-escaping machine, a portable bathing machine, a cure for smoking chimneys, a swinging machine for the benefit of health, a roasting machine and a cork-bottomed lifeboat. He never patented any of his inventions however and, in the case of his lifeboat, someone else took the credit for the device.

With his interest in invention, his love of novelty, and his eagerness to attract more people to his museum, Crosthwaite's discovery of music

Advertisement for a Richardson's Concert in Worcester in 1846

within the stones around Skiddaw must have been met with great excitement. In his memorandum book he records the day of his discovery:
The entry reads: 'June 11th, 1785 found my 6 first music stones at the Tip end or North end of long tongue.'

He told people that the first six notes he found on that day were in perfect tune; the remaining ten of the set took six months to find, with Crosthwaite working twelve hours a day to tune them, carefully chipping away at the stone until the desired note rang true. He carved into each stone the letter corresponding to the note which the stone sounded. The result was a sort of xylophone, known as 'Musical Stones'. Within his museum, which was situated at Museum Square at the bottom of Keswick's Market Place, Crosthwaite set up a series of mirrors near the windows so that he could see whenever a carriage was approaching. When a carriage neared, he would bang out a rudimentary tune on his Musical Stones and his daughter and 'the old woman' banged a drum, rattled a Chinese gong and a played a barrel organ. This cacophony of noise pouring out of the museum was meant to attract the attention of the carriage passengers and any people passing on the street so they might come and look round.

It is unlikely that Peter Crosthwaite could have predicted how, 55 years later, his initial discovery led to international fame and royal acclaim for the next exponent of the Musical

Obelisk Monument to Joseph and Samuel Richardson. Photograph reproduced by kind permission of the Friends of Kensal Green Cemetery.

Stones, Mr Joseph Richardson.

Joseph Richardson was born in 1790 and was a stonemason from a family of Keswick stonemasons. He was something of a musical genius and made numerous musical instruments in his youth. The Cumberland and Westmorland Herald reported in 1928 that Joseph once took his mother's mahogany-topped table 'of which she was very proud' and sawed it up to make a violin! As well as conducting his own experiments, it is very likely that as a child Joseph would have been familiar with Crosthwaite's Musical Stones. During his career as a stonemason Richardson noticed for himself the curious musical ring given out by some rocks when struck. Consequently he began to test the various rocks of the Lake District for their note and collected ones that gave a pure, resonant ring, forming them into a sequence.

In 1827, whilst building houses at Thornthwaite, he found that the rocks of Skiddaw had the best tone of all and, spurred on by this discovery, he endeavoured to produce an instrument on a larger scale than Crosthwaite's, which would have every musical note. The geological name for the rock both Crosthwaite and Richardson used for their instruments is 'hornfel'. It took Richardson almost thirteen years to collect and shape enough individual notes of hornfel to make an eight-octave range. By day he would scour the hillside looking for suitable stones, then bring them the long distance home where he would work tirelessly to cut and shape them. It was a colossal task: Joseph experimented at length with each stone before accepting or rejecting it as worthy of the instrument he was constructing. The massive task of assembling this instrument consumed Joseph absolutely, so much so that he and his family were reduced to poverty through this 13-year period. He found it hard to carry on at times but eventually in 1840 the instrument was finished.

Joseph enlisted his three sons and they began practising with the instrument and giving concerts locally. Joseph was a gifted self-taught musician who was proficient on the violin, flute and pipes. He was able to use his musical abilities to get the most out of his Musical Stones and train his sons to assist him in building an impressive repertoire. Having gained support and acclaim in the Keswick region they set off in 1840 on a three-week tour of the major northern towns of England. Their reception and immediate success meant that they did not see their home again for three years. One local newspaper noted that everyone appeared much delighted with the 'sweet sound' elicited from the rugged, uncouth looking and unique instrument. Their success encouraged them to head for London, where 'the wonderful merits of your admirable instrument cannot fail to be well-received by the London public who are very musical people.'

The repertoire included selections from Handel, Beethoven and Mozart and arrangements of waltzes, quadrilles, gallops and polkas. Considerable variation in tone was achieved by using different methods of striking the notes, creating a blend of organ, piano, harp and flute sounds, though the full power of the instrument had to be withheld because of the fear of shattering the concert hall windows. The concerts were immensely popular: 'The richness as well as the sweetness of the tones produced seemed to excite the astonishment of all who heard them.' In an 1846 newspaper advertisement for the Richardsons' performance in Luton, it states that the range of the instrument went from the 'alleged warble of a lark' to the 'deep bass of a funeral bell'. In an amusingly florid newspaper piece written in 1842 the journalist Minnie Broatch explains that Richardson's set of Musical Stones 'looks more or less like one of those toys children play with, which are called dulcimers in the toy shops, but on a gargantuan scale - they would be for giant children to play with if they were in reality a child's toy . . .'

To increase the musical range the instrument was updated in the mid 1840s with octaves of steel bars, Swiss bells, drums and various instruments of percussion, and became 'Richardson & Sons, Rock, Bell and Steel Band.' On 23rd February 1848 the Richardsons played at Buckingham Palace, by command of Queen Victoria. Prince Albert was present, and a large assembly of English and foreign noblemen and women. The Band was well received; indeed, two of the pieces were requested for an encore. According to The Times, it proved 'one of the most extraordinary and novel performances of the Metropolis'. As a result, the Queen requested two further performances. However, although very impressed overall, it was noted that Her Majesty was not amused by the sound of the Alpine bells.

Over sixty concerts were given in London alone and the Band toured all over Britain and subsequently in France, Germany and Italy, being transported by train. A concert trip to America was planned, but Robert, the youngest son and the most talented player, became ill just before the date of departure and died of pneumonia. The tour was abandoned, and the

Brian Dewan, Jamie Barnes and Ted Dewan playing the Stones across to Brantwood. Photo courtesy of Paul Wilson.

instrument was packed away. Subsequently, the instrument was given to Keswick Museum in 1917 by the great-grandson of Joseph Richardson. It still stands there now, as a symbol of the stonemason from Crosthwaite, his natural musical talent and his tremendous drive to achieve the goal of creating an instrument from rock that had every musical note.

Joseph Richardson is buried at Kensal Green Cemetery in London. As well as a gravestone, Joseph also has a monument there to mark his life and his achievement. The monument is the tallest obelisk in the cemetery and it reads: 'In Memory of Joseph Richardson, formerly of Underskiddaw, Keswick, Cumberland. Inventor of the Instruments of the Rock, Bell and Steel Band.'

Later sets of Musical Stones include the Till Family Rock Band, exhibited and performed by Daniel Till of Keswick and his two sons in 1881 at the Crystal Palace. It later toured America and is now held in the Metropolitan Museum, New York. The Abraham Brothers of Keswick, famous for their mountaineering and photography, collected a set of fifty-eight stones in the late nineteenth century, which took them twelve years and which they exhibited in their photography shop on Lake Road. But of all the lithophones, the 'Richardson & Sons Rock, Bell & Steel Band' was the most celebrated.

The Richardsons stopped touring with the Musical Stones more than 140 years ago. However, recent musical collaborations have meant that the Stones have started to go on tour once more, and a further series of concert appearances are planned over the next few years. The first of these 21st century Musical Stones tours took place in September of 2005. Keswick Museum was approached by Grizedale Arts - a contemporary art commissioning agency near Coniston - to collaborate with the musician and artist Brian Dewan from Brooklyn, New York. Jamie Barnes, the Duty Officer at Keswick Museum, worked with Brian over a number of weeks and assisted him in composing seven 'movements' for the Musical Stones. This suite of music lasted about an hour and was performed outdoors on the shore of Coniston Water, looking out across the lake towards Brantwood, the former home of the great writer, artist and social reformer John Ruskin. Ruskin had been so impressed by the Musical Stones that he had commissioned a set to be made for him personally. He remarked that the Stones had given him 'a new musical pleasure'.

The lakeside performance by Brian and Jamie was part of the Coniston Water Festival 2005, a country sports and art festival which had been restarted by Grizedale Arts to allow the local community to take over the continuation of the event from 2007 onwards.

A special frame and sound-box was constructed to mount the stones on for the performance. Brian used 35 of the 61 slate notes for his composition. These notes correspond to the white notes on a piano. The performance was amplified and the sounds of the stones drifted across the lake and into Coniston village.

There were more performances in 2006 on the Stones further afield: a repeat of the Coniston music in Leeds, and some new music at the Liverpool Biennial with a classical Chinese orchestra. In January 2006 the Musical Stones reached a large national audience when they were heavily featured in a BBC Radio 4 documentary on Cumbrian musical stones presented by the top classical percussionist Evelyn Glennie. The documentary was entitled 'The World's First Rock Band'.

In addition, Keswick Museum and Art Gallery are also involved with a major three-year research project set up by Leeds University entitled 'Ruskin Rocks'. This is an interdisciplinary project to find out why hornfel

Evelyn Glennie and Jamie Barnes

has musical properties, to carry out historical and literary research on the Cumbrian sets of musical stones and organise a series of performances.

Keswick Museum hopes that all these new projects will help bring the Musical Stones to new audiences and keep this fascinating story alive for another 220 years at least.

Further reading:
M.C. Fagg: *Rock Music*, Pitt Rivers Museum, ISBN 0 902793 39 X

**HENRY COWPER MARSHALL (1808 - 1884)
The man, his family and an island**

Margaret Armstrong

The hollow wooden sound of oars in rowlocks, the steely surface of the lake, pebbles seen through clear water as she dabbled her fingers over the side of a rowing boat, are impressions recorded in her *Memories* by eighty-one year old Frances Partridge. She was one of the granddaughters of Henry Cowper Marshall. Born in 1900 she never knew her grandfather who died in 1884 nor did she know her father William's older brother John who inherited the house on Derwent Island. She was visiting his widow 'spherical old Aunt Ernestine' twenty years after his death in 1894. Frances also wrote of the garden stretching to the water's edge instead of to a wall or road and the novelty of having to take a boat to go shopping in the town of Keswick. In this expedition she was following most of Henry's children, grandchildren and relatives who through the years since his purchase of the property in 1844 had made their summer pilgrimage to this romantic place.

Henry was born in 1808, the fourth son of John Marshall (1765-1845), a Leeds manufacturer of linen thread and his wife Jane (1770-1847). John's father died young leaving him a drapery business and a legacy that he used to set up a factory and develop a method of spinning flax by machine. By using the researches of all his associates and with the foresight that led him to buy when raw material was cheap and stock it until there was demand during and after the wars with France, he built more factories and made a massive fortune. John Marshall was perhaps the most successful northern entrepreneur of his time and one of the first self-made men to rival the aristocracy with his wealth.

At the age of thirty, in 1795, John Marshall married Jane, a distant cousin, the fifth daughter of William Pollard, a Halifax merchant. They shared the same school and Unitarian religious background. Dorothy Wordsworth was for some time Jane's companion at Hipperholme School in Halifax. The later close friendship with Dorothy and William Wordsworth, together with the fact that John and Jane spent a three week honeymoon in the Lake District is likely to have influenced John Marshall when he began to invest money in land and houses there.

The estates of the Mounseys, the so called Kings of Patterdale, was one of the purchases he had made by the end of the French wars. There, on the western shore of Ullswater, John Marshall built Hallsteads to be his summer home. He loved the situation looking across the lake to the Martindale Fells and his great joy was walking amongst the crags and rowing on the shining water, especially in the moonlight. Much of this pleasure must have been shared in their formative years by his younger children and would influence them when the opportunity came to choose a location for their own summer residences.

Henry entered the family firm in 1828. His interest was not in the technical side of the work but in the commercial aspect of the operation. He devised brilliant and highly efficient systems of recording stock and turnover. John Marshall was still in control but Henry's two older brothers John II and James Garth were partners.

The social circumstances and the expectations that Henry grew up with were very different from the modest childhood that his father had known. In 1821 John Marshall was High Sheriff of Cumberland and in the same year he rented a house in London partly for business reasons and partly so that the family might enjoy the London season. Eventually he entered

Parliament. He was a Whig and the first Yorkshire mill-owner to become a member. Through the connections and prestige so conferred, the family made many new and useful acquaintances. It was probably in this setting that Henry Cowper Marshall met the young woman who would become his wife.

Catherine Lucy Spring-Rice was the youngest daughter of Thomas Spring-Rice, first Baron Monteagle, Chancellor of the Exchequer in Lord Melbourne's government from 1835-1839. The marriage in 1838 was a source of gratification for John and Jane Marshall and Henry soon became prominent in Leeds liberal circles. First he was an Alderman of the city and then Lord Mayor in 1843. A portrait from that time, provided by the Yorkshire Archive Service shows him not looking as might be expected of a Lord Mayor of Leeds. He seems youthful for a thirty-five year old. Long hair tumbles around a serious face and the mayoral chain is worn over a high necked shirt and a jacket with undone buttons. He was drawing a considerable income from the firm and had a substantial home for his growing family at Weetwood Hall on the outskirts of Leeds. This then, was the time to embark on a new venture motivated in part by circumstances befalling his close knit family.

As John Marshall bought more and more land in the Lake District, he encouraged and often financed his sons so that they could do likewise. In 1828 he gave Patterdale Hall to his eldest son, William. He was a lawyer, expected to inherit the country estates and except probably in an advisory capacity had no connection with the firm. John II entered the business when he was seventeen and within five years was given capital and made a partner. He married into minor gentry. His wife, Mary Ballantyne Dykes of Dovenby Hall, near Cockermouth came from an old Cumberland family. John Marshall built John and Mary a house in Leeds and was looking around for a country property for them when the Castlerigg Estate at Keswick came on the market. It had been forfeited to the crown when the Earl of Derwentwater was beheaded for his part in the Jacobite Rebellion of 1715 and subsequently given to Greenwich Hospital. William Wordsworth was anxious that his friend should buy the land and keep it intact. He was concerned that if it fell into the wrong hands it would become streets of lodging houses, stables and inns. In 1832, partly financed by his father, John II became Lord of the Manor of Castlerigg. It was understood that he would build a fine house on the east shore of

Derwentwater, at Broomhill Point. A prominent architect of the time, Anthony Salvin prepared a set of plans.

The town of Keswick was expanding in a southerly direction and there was concern that the parish church of Crosthwaite was too far to the north. The Reverend J. Bush, a curate of Crosthwaite began to hold services in the Town Hall. John Marshall II perceived that it was inadequate and after trying to share the task with others, decided to take upon himself the building of a new church for the town. The plans for his house were abandoned. For the church he chose a magnificent site, where an old windmill had stood on a hilltop and asked Salvin to prepare plans for a building in the Old English style. In 1836, when the foundations had just been laid John became ill and died in London. There was a great sense of shock and devastation. Apart from one daughter who lived only a year, John and Jane Marshall had reared all their offspring. 'Never surely was there a mother who had so little sorrow in the bringing up of eleven children' Dorothy Wordsworth had once written to Jane.

The Castlerigg Estate passed to Reginald Dykes Marshall, the six year old son of John II. The Marshall family decided that the building of the church should continue. It is feasible to think that they felt it would be a fitting memorial. Mary paid the full cost of the building, £4103, and in 1838 the church was opened. Shortly afterwards her husband's remains were brought from London and interred in the nave. Henry Cowper Marshall was one of the guardians of Reginald and acted for him when his mother made him Patron of the living. He is likely to have been in Keswick frequently as the church of St John the Evangelist and the parsonage funded by the Marshall family was being built. Correspondence shows that he monitored closely the progress of the work to ensure that it proceeded according to contract. In 1842 Henry's youngest sister, Susan moved into the parsonage when she married the widower, Henry Myers, the brilliant young cleric appointed as the first incumbent. How often through these years did Henry Cowper Marshall stand looking over the islands of Derwentwater to Catbells and beyond? The incomparable beauty of the ranks of fells, different according to time and season must have seeped into his soul. In 1844 the most northerly island was for sale. Fate seemed to have taken a hand. He bought it.

In the 12th century Derwent Island was part of the lands owned by Furness Abbey and called Hestholm (Horse Island). After the dissolution of the monasteries it was granted to a John Williamson of Crosthwaite, who sold it for £60 to the Mines Royal. The German miners working copper mines in the district for Queen Elizabeth, had three hundred fruit trees, a brewhouse, a bakery and a windmill on the island. The foreigners were not popular with the local people and it was a refuge for them.

By 1650 the miners had gone and all was in ruins. In 1778, Joseph Pocklington, a Nottinghamshire banker with a vast fortune bought the island. He employed locals Samuel and Thomas Ladyman to build him a Palladian mansion in the centre of the seven acre island and to put up a number of mock antique follies around the shore. William Wordsworth was disgusted with the despoiling of the natural landscape by an 'alien improver'. The next owner was Lt Col William Peachey MP. He pulled down most of the follies and diversified the planting, thinning out the dense clumps of fir trees. It was from Peachey's widow that Henry Cowper Marshall bought Derwent Island and began enthusiastically to make it the social centre for his extended family. He employed Anthony Salvin to enlarge the house, making a new dining room, a loggia and extra bedrooms. A service wing was created for the servants, often brought from Leeds. New furniture, loosely copying 18th century styles was collected or specially made. The gardens were landscaped and many fine trees planted. Water pipes were laid beneath the lake and there was a fleet of boats to carry people and provisions to and from Keswick.

Coincidences occurred to bring the family even closer together. In 1841 James Garth Marshall, married Mary Spring-Rice, the sister of Henry's wife and a few months later, the widower Thomas Spring-Rice, Lord Mounteagle married Henry's oldest sister Marianne. John and Jane Marshall were failing in health and it would seem that the new house on Derwent Island became the focus for family gatherings. Groups of nephews, nieces and cousins moved around between Hallsteads, Patterdale Hall and James Garth Marshall's house at Monk Coniston. Wealthy and privileged, they enjoyed the natural surroundings and the fine books and paintings that stocked all the houses, but undoubtedly Henry's summer home had the most exciting position. It is said that each year he recorded the height and weight of all the growing children of the family. To discourage common trippers, he bought up more islands and land all around Derwentwater and strongly opposed a proposal to build a railway to Ambleside.

Catherine died in 1853 after giving Henry four sons: John III who was to inherit the island house; Stephen who made a home at Skelwith Fold;Francis, a schoolmaster, who in retirement built a house at Hawse End; and William, an architect. The latter designed the extension of the chancel of St. John's church in 1889 and incorporated the oak choir stalls as a memorial to his father. Affixed to the choir stalls is the dedication, 'Henry Cowper Marshall. To whose care and forethought worshippers of this church are much indebted.'

Many more people were destined to be indebted to Henry for having followed his heart and purchased Derwent Island. After nearly forty golden years, the property passed to John III and then in 1894 to his second son John IV. By this time money taken out and mismanagement led to the failure of the firm and the fragmentation of the family fortunes.

John Marshall IV, a bachelor, lame and in poor health spent much of his time at the home on Derwent Island. He it was who embellished the drawing room with elegant wood and plasterwork and continued to welcome relations and friends, including some who would eventually influence the fate of the property. Sir Robert Hunter, Canon Rawnsley and Octavia Hill were frequent visitors and from their discussions came the idea of forming a national trust. John IV died in 1923. In St John's Church, the children he would have loved to have, are shown grouped around Jesus, in the beautiful memorial window by the arts and crafts movement designer, Veronica Whall.

For almost another thirty years the island home would be in the care of the brothers of John IV, first Charles and then Denis. More than one hundred years after Henry Cowper Marshall first set foot on Derwent Island, in 1951 Denis gave it to the National Trust. Preservation and maintenance are carried out by the Trust and by their carefully chosen tenants. There are trippers but not in the hoards that would have horrified Henry. On a limited number of summer afternoons, members of the public are ferried over to walk in the steps of the Marshall family and imagine a life that has gone. The natural beauty of Derwent Island is timeless.

Henry Cowper Marshall has a solid memorial, a pseudo-Celtic sandstone cross about eight feet high, only yards from the path he would have walked many times between the church of St. John and the parsonage. Sons and grandsons are more discreetly remembered. They lie beside him in moss-covered graves almost lost amongst the undergrowth. For the preservation of open land and many of the mature trees we enjoy today, Keswick people owe Henry and the Marshall family much more than they know.

Further reading :-
W. G. Rimmer: *Marshalls of Leeds Flax Spinners (1788-1886)*, Cambridge University Press. 1960
Francis Partridge: *Memories*, 1981
Margaret Armstrong: *Linen and Liturgy - The Story of the Marshall Family and the Parish Church of Keswick St. John,* Peel Wyke Publications. 2002
The National Trust Guide to Derwent Island.

JOHN RICHARDSON (1817 - 1886)
Waller, builder, schoolmaster and dialect poet
'A poet of the people'

Brian Wilkinson

Tuesday, 4th May 1886. A large crowd of mourners follow the coffin of John Richardson in the ancient single-horse hearse up the steep and narrow road to the church of St John, high on Naddle above the Vale of St John. Young and old, farmers and their wives, in their Sunday best, farm servants and labourers, officers of the Cumberland Association for the Advancement of Literature and Science, to whom John had often lectured, folk from Keswick, Threlkeld and beyond, had come to give their respects to this old man who had rarely left his native vale. The vicar leads the

Above: John Richardson (Image courtesy of Keswick Museum)

party, pausing occasionally to allow the old horse to get its breath.

John was taking his final journey; to be buried in the churchyard of the church he had rebuilt some forty years before, a fitting venue for his final resting place. Until 1865 St John's had been a chapel of ease, one of five with the mother church at Crosthwaite, Keswick and serving the farming community of the Vale of St John. Now St John's was a parish in its own right, together with the even smaller church at Wythburn.

The funeral procession included many well-known local folk, in addition to numerous relatives. Many friends came from Keswick and Threlkeld, Wythburn, the Brunskills from Threlkeld Vicarage, the Croziers from the Riddings, and the Wilsons from the prestigious Keswick Hotel, walking up the steep hill from Bridge House, home to John and his family for some twenty-eight years, to the church next to the school, in which he had served as schoolmaster.

F. J. Carruthers maintains that 'No church in the diocese has a more dramatic setting; more spectacular surroundings .... no church in the county holds better the shape and the spirit of the church which it replaced.' The chapel which John Richardson rebuilt was erected at a time when new churches were being built in towns and cities across the land with soaring steeples and graceful aisles. Not so for John Richardson. His new chapel was 'plain, low and small with a miniature tower at the west that is not much bigger than a chimney'. It is a delight to see, and fitted perfectly in its situation among the rugged crags and extensive views of the northern Lakes scenery. If anything, it was a reflection of John

St John's Church

St John's School (now the Diocesan Youth Centre)

Richardson's character, and all the better for it.

The church was of an ancient foundation, possibly founded as a hostel by the Knights Hospitallers of St John as a traveller's refuge. The hostel became, in time, an inn, and with the chapel, which was founded later, became the centre of the life of a wide rural area. Today it appears remote - with the old school ideal for its present use as the Diocesan Youth Centre where young and old come to enjoy the countryside - but it lies on an ancient track from the Vale of Eden, over the northern slopes of Helvellyn and on to Castlerigg and Keswick to the west - with both chapel and school convenient in situation for the scattered community which it served.

Where the track levels, before the descent to Dalebottom, lies the church and school, both of which would forever be associated with the man who was making his last journey on this earth. Most men aim to achieve something in their lives. Some are remembered for one or perhaps two achievements. John Richardson realised success in three spheres, as a 'waller' and builder, a schoolmaster and a dialect writer of both poetry and prose, an equal among the many dialect writers born and bred in his native county of Cumberland, or 'Cummerlan' as he would have it.

John Richardson was born on the 4th May, 1817, at Stone House, a lonely cottage on the western slopes of Naddle, the long rocky fell that divides the Vale of St John from Dalebottom. He was baptised at St John's Chapel on 6th October.

John and his wife Grace had nine children, of whom eight survived infancy, four sons and four daughters. Some of his children moved away from the Vale, with the eldest emigrating to New Zealand where he became a senior banker. A second son became manager of a Brighton business and the others gained responsible positions in Derbyshire and Liverpool. They were raised and taught well.

John was brought up by his father as a waller and mason. Wallers were the craftsmen who built the drystone walls that march across the landscape of the Lake District - built to last a hundred years or more. Early in his working life John began to build houses, cottages and farm buildings in the Vale of St John and in Keswick. He was the builder who built the vicarage at Dalebottom and in Keswick he had built several houses, the most distinguished perhaps being the terrace at Derwentwater Place, opposite the Keswick St John's Church and which has now been refurbished to provide apartments, without altering the handsome façade. In addition to the church, John built the school some four years later.

John was a mason and builder for some twenty-five years. Then, his state of health demanded that he take more sedentary work and he became headmaster of the school he had built, living at Bridge House in the Vale of St John for another twenty-seven years until his retirement some eleven months before his death.

At the age of twenty-four years John married Grace, the beautiful daughter of John and Grace Birkett of City House, Wythburn. The house was part of the hamlet called 'The City' which now lies under the waters of Thirlmere, a reservoir for Manchester, built at the end of the nineteenth century.

John's best-remembered poem, 'It's Nobbut Me!' is said to be the story of his courtship. John's courting days entailed a long walk from Stone House to 'The City', some five miles or so. There would have been occasional social gatherings where young men met their future wives, but John decided that the girl he wanted to marry was worth the effort involved.

His courtship of Grace, the youngest of a family of twelve, is told with humour and tenderness in what is regarded as one of the best pieces of Cumbrian dialect poetry printed - and told from the girl's point of view. It seems that it was an old Cumberland custom to 'jike' or knock on the window of a young girl at night to gain admittance to the house for 'a spot of courtin'.

It's Nobbut Me!

Ya winter neet; I mind it weel,
Oor lads hed been at t' fell,
An', bein' tir't, went seun to bed,
An' I sat be messel'.
I hard a jike on t' window pane,
An' deftly went to see;
An' when I ax't, 'Who's jiken theer?'
Says t' chap, 'It's nobbut me!'
'Who's me?' says I, 'What want ye here?
Oor fwok ur aw i' bed;' -
'I dunnet want your fwok at aw,
It's thee I want' he sed.
'What cant'e want wi' me', says I;
'An' who, the deuce, can't be?
Just tell me who it is, an' than'-
Says he, 'It's nobbut me'.
'I want a sweetheart, an' I thowt
Thoo mebby wad an' aw;
I'd been a bit down t'deal to-neet
An' thowt 'at I wad caw;
What, cant'e like me, dus t'e think?
I think I wad like thee' -
'I dunnet know who 't is,' says I,
Says he, 'It's nobbut me.'
We pestit on a canny while,
I thowt his voice I kent;
An' then I steal quite whisht away,
An' oot at t' dooer I went.
I creap, an' gat him be t'cwoat laps,
'Twas dark, he cuddent see;
He startit roond, an' said, 'Who's that?'

Says I, 'It's nobbut me'.
An' menny a time he com agean,
An' menny a time I went,
An' sed, 'Who's that jiken theer?'
When gaily weel I kent:
An' mainly what t'seam answer com,
Fra back o' laylick tree;
He sed, 'I think thoo knows who't is:
Thoo knows it's nobbut me'.
It's twenty year an' mair sen than,
An' ups an' doons we've hed;
An six fine barns hev blest us beath,
Sen Jim and me war wed.
An' menny a time I've known him steal,
When I'd yan on my knee,
To mak me start, an' than wad laugh -
  'Ha! Ha! It's nobbut me'.

John was well regarded as a scholar. His contributions to the Cumberland Association for the Advancement of Literature and Science included papers on the Cumbrian Dialect, Old Customs and Usages of the Lake District, Superstitions Once Common in the Lake District, Sports and Pastimes in the Lake Country, Cumberland before the Union with Scotland, Scottish Life and Character, and Dialects of the Lake Country. Scholarship was always highly regarded in rural Cumberland - and often the priest was the schoolmaster too. There was, and still is, a close relationship with Queen's College at Oxford and the twin counties of Cumberland and Westmorland and young people from this part of the country can still be found among the undergraduates there.

In 1839 John's lecture to the Society was 'Stwories 'at Granny Used to Tell', being sketches of life in the Cumbrian valleys in the early nineteenth century, scenes and incidents that actually happened, narrated to John by Grace's mother at Wythburn before she died, aged ninety-five years.

John began to write poetry in dialect at an early age and published at intervals in the local press. At the age of 54 years, in 1871, he published 'Cummerlan' Talk' and in 1876 a second volume. Cowards of Carlisle were his publishers. It was an immediate success, and reprinted in 1874, 1876 and 1886. In its day, it was a 'best seller' and justifiably so. It was said that a copy could be found in every farmhouse in the county.

The organist William Metcalf of Carlisle Cathedral set two of John's poems to music, 'It's Nobbut Me!' and 'John Crozier's Talley Ho!' (John Crozier was Master of the Blencathra Hunt for sixty-four years). Metcalf's setting of Woodcock Graves' 'D'ye Ken John Peel?' eclipsed the 'Talley Ho!' in popularity, but 'It's Nobbut Me!' continued to be performed as a drawing room ballad for many years.

F. J. Carruthers in his *Lore of the Lake Country* refers to the magical qualities of the Vale of St John and adds 'but its real magic came from the mind and the pen of John Richardson whose dialect poetry has a delicacy and tenderness which nobody else has been able to draw from a folk speech which seems to have been designed for fratching and fighting, since it contains no fewer than one hundred and nine words meaning 'beating' or sixty-seven ways of calling a man (or a woman) a fool'.

Indeed, John himself is at pains to point out in his introduction to 'Cummerlan' Talk' that his readers would not find 'descriptions of rude or riotous scenes, similar to those described by Anderson, Stagg [dialect writers of an earlier era] or some others of the Cumberland bards …. and the half century which has passed away since they wrote has brought a great and beneficial change in the manners and customs of the Cumberland rural population'.

The Cumbrian dialect was, of course, the native tongue of John. As he once put it, he could talk 'polite' to visitors. By this he meant not 'politely' but 'properly'. John was ever courteous to everyone he met. In 1884, nearly forty years after the rebuilding of the chapel, and long retired from schoolmastering, he spoke to a curious visitor. The churchyard was being enlarged for the first time since it was first used for burials some one hundred and fifty years before. The visitor ventured to suggest that it had first been consecrated in about 1730. John disagreed, maintaining that the consecration took place some twenty years before that date. The visitor enquired if anyone had died in that twenty-year period. Oh yes, said John, but it was a common belief that the Devil was ready to claim the first body buried there. Who was the first to be buried there and risked being taken by the Devil? No one knew. Perhaps it was a tramp found dead by the roadside!

When building the new wall to the extension of the graveyard, stone from the ruins of the ancient inn were used. John must have cast an expert eye over the new drystone wall and declared it 'As fine a bit of work in that line as I ever saw - even on the fells'. The inn had been mentioned in James Clark's 'Survey of the Lakes' in 1794. John Richardson had a fine sense of humour, and loved to quote Defoe's well-known quatrain

> *Wherever God erects a house of prayer,*
> *The Devil always builds a chapel there;*
> *And 'twill be found upon examination,*
> *The latter has the largest congregation.*

The quotation from Defoe also applied to the little church at Wythburn, Wordsworth's 'modest house of prayer', all that is left of the hamlet called 'The City', apart from West Head Farm and several cottages, now drowned under the waters of Thirmere. Here the 'Devil's chapel' was The Nag's Head Inn, not drowned but demolished almost within living memory because Manchester Corporation thought that the drains from the inn would pollute the reservoir.

The Reverend Wilfred Braithwaite conducted the Dialect Services of the Lakeland Dialect Society until his death in 2002. In one of his services Wilfred Braithwaite spoke of John Richardson. 'He was a man who saw dialect not merely as a rough and ready way of speaking, not as uneducated or uncultivated English badly pronounced. He saw it as a way of speaking that is much older than the current speech. John Richardson saw that our dialect could tell us a great deal about the dalesfolk of long ago, even since Celtic times. The Lakeland Dialect Society thrives today, with over three hundred members, several from abroad.

Two local authors, one from the nineteenth century and one from the twentieth, described John Richardson in detail. In 'Chapters from the English Lakes' H. D. Rawnsley wrote of him as 'another poet since Scott's day who has made its scenery …. his own'. Rawnsley knew John Richardson well and often talked with him. He describes him as 'well and strongly built, with the face of an elderly man who has found the peace that is bred from adversity. With a fine, open forehead, lined with care but most with thought, grey 'Viking' eyes that have a dreamy far-away look about them; a face solid and reposeful enough, but filled with soul and with benevolence; a mouth that is closely set, except when by a twinkle in the eye, you feel the man has laughter at his heart'.

In a more recent context, F. J. Carruthers describes John as 'the supreme example of one of the popular images of the Lake County dalesmen - quiet, resolute, kind-hearted and self-effacing ....his work .... is characteristic of all that is known about him; the product of a thoughtful heart and a sympathetic mind. He did not aim high: his quest for ideas seldom took him beyond the actual experiences of his life or the tranquil scenes in which he moved .... he wrote only of the placid life that he knew; the life for which he had wished when he was young, and which he knew he had achieved when he reached old age.... simply bred, he lived to the end of his life in sturdy independence of spirit, but with absolute modesty both of manner and of wants, and having few things - home, work, wife and bairns, a bit of garden ground, a good conscience and the exquisite beauty of the vale and hill to quicken and inspire him and with a few good standard books close to hand - he was therewithal content'.

We are grateful to John Richardson for his accurate account of Old Cumberland 'wises' and doings, as given us in 'T' barring out', 'What used to be lang sen', 'A Crack about Auld Times' and his 'Stwories Granny used to Tell'. But for John Richardson, we should not have known about the 'auld fashint' weddins' and buryins', 'auld fashint' farmers' or 'sec winters they hed lang sen' - and the early days of the last century would have been a sealed book'.

John recounts in 'Cummerlan' Talk' the old Cumbrian custom of 'Barrin' Oot'. It seems that 'barrin' oot' or preventing the schoolmaster from entering the school building was not unknown in old Cumbria - and not entirely frowned on. But, the custom died out many years ago, perhaps accelerated in its demise when a local schoolmaster lost an eye in the fracas, though not at St John's.

''Oh! Man, bit theer's been a deal o' ups an' doons sen I went t'scheul. I's abeun sebbenty noo, an' it'll be mair ner fifty years sen than.' So begins John Richardson's classic tale of the time when he and his fellow scholars 'barred oot' the schoolmaster. The scholars had decided that they wanted an extra holiday and some remission of holiday tasks (homework was an unpopular then as now!) - or just felt the need for some devilment to enliven the school day. The plan was to keep the schoomaster out of the school building until their demands were met.

'Priest Wilson' was the schoolmaster at St John's in those days - and regarded as a very good schoolmaster too. He was sometimes sharp with the boys and some of 't' laal uns' were frightened to death of him. Twenty or more of the scholars were 'girt fellows', almost men, and they egged each other in behaviour causing the schoolmaster to tighten up on his discipline or lose control - and that would never do.

John's reflections of 'barrin' oot' days were that they occurred when the Christmas or the midsummer holidays were coming. As soon as the schoolmaster had left the building to have his dinner the boys would set to work. They wrote their 'demands' on a piece of paper, ready to put through the keyhole when the schoolmaster returned, demanding a week's extra holiday and 'neagh tasks'. If the scholars did manage to keep the master out they would usually get all or most of what they wanted. But, if the master managed to get into the school the boys would slink off to their desks, 'hinging their lugs', smarting from the punishment they had been given. Then a 'gay lang task' would be given for the holidays, and maybe a good hiding as well.

John remembered the midsummer when he and his fellow scholars were determined to bar the master from the school. They had all contrived to have their dinners (their 'bait') with them on that day and began to work on the barricades as soon as the master had stepped over the threshold on his way home.

They had three or four large tubs ready and as soon as the master was out of sight they brought them into the school. They fetched water from the school dam and filled the tubs. They were not too particular about the cleanliness of the water - 'It was gailey weel mix't wid meud an' dirt.' The boys then made 'swirts o' kesks' [the hollow stems of cow parsley] to squirt water into the master's face if he tried to get in at the windows. The door was barred next, the window casements nailed down and everything made as secure as possible. Then, they ate their 'bait' and waited for the master to return.

When the master did come back from his dinner he saw immediately what they had done and shouted 'varra ill-natur't like' for the scholars to open the door. The boys retaliated by pushing the paper through the keyhole 'demandin' oor reets.' The master was furious and went off for help. The boys thought that perhaps he had gone for good but they kept a sharp lookout. Then the master reappeared with reinforcements - 'girt' Joe Thompson from Sykes Farm with his man-servant Isaac Todd. They had come armed with 'gavelocks' (iron crowbars) and 'girt hammers' over their shoulders. At this sight the scholars were 'gaily flait' (very frightened). Joe 'was a girt lump of a fellow'. He was 'as strong as a cuddy' (donkey). He was the right man for the job.

The situation was beginning to look serious for the scholars, but they could see no way but to continue the fight. So, when one the raiding party came beneath a window, the boys let fly with their 'swirts' and half drowned him with dirty water. They drove them back in that way many times, but the raiders always managed to rally and eventually broke the window with a fearful smash. For all that they couldn't get into the school. The scholars rammed anything else they could find into the broken casement and squirted water until they fell back.

It was quiet for a while and the scholars thought that they had repelled the raiders for good. But, they found out later that Isaac Todd had gone to fetch some cans, and it wasn't long before all three, Isaac, Joe and the Priest himself began throwing water through the hole in the window so quickly that the scholars feared they would be 'droon't oot.'

For a time the scholars were dumbfounded, but then their 'mettle was fairly up' and they decided to make a sortie outside. They rushed out of the door and threatened to put the raiders into the school dam. Two or three of them did get hold of Isaac Todd and threw him in head first. About twenty lads got hold of 'girt Joe' but he held on to the gatepost and they couldn't shift him. So, they set off like a pack of hounds in full cry after the Priest. But Priest Wilson was a 'lish fellow' in those days and could keep up a rattling pace for many a mile. He took off for Low Rigg and soon the scholars lost sight of him - and to tell the truth they weren't sorry that they couldn't catch him.

The scholars had won the day, and you may be sure they made no little noise about it. There were thirty or forty gathered together, boasting of what great feats they had done. By this time it was mid-afternoon. The scholars set to work to tidy and repair the school as best they could. Then they made a collection between themselves for cash prizes and held a sports, with wrestling, foot racing and 'lowpin and leapin' on the green just above the school. One thing that made them 'gaily proud' was that the schoolmaster and Joe Thompson came back and joined them and all passed off as right as could be.

The scholars heard no more of Isaac Todd that day. They thought that 'mebbe he had gone yam and t' bed' until his clothes were dry and fit to put on again.

And in such a way ended 'T' Barrin' Oot!'

John did not always enjoy good heath and it was a relief to become a schoolmaster rather than continue a builder's work in later life. And so, for some twenty-seven years he was teaching, writing, lecturing - and fishing in St John's Beck. It was a satisfying life - and no 'barrin' oot'!

After eleven years of retirement, John was seen to stumble and fall on the 29th April whilst walking down to Bridge House, and died the following day.

In his last months of illness, Stafford Howard, the Carlisle poet Robert Ferguson, the Bishop of Carlisle and the Keswick writer and journalist Eliza Lynn Linton all attempted to have John awarded a literary pension, but to no avail. John Richardson left a legacy of prose and poetry that will live for as long as Cumbrians and those from further afield appreciate his 'mak o' Cummerlan' Talk'.

Further reading:
F. J. Carruthers: *Lore of the Lake Country*, Robert Hale, 1975
John Richardson: *Cummerlan' Talk*, G & T Coward, Carlisle, 1871
H. D. Rawnsley: *Chapters At The English Lakes*, Maclehose, Jackson & Co, Glasgow, 1913

Acknowledgements:
Thanks to Rev. Geoffrey Darrell (former Vicar) and Rev. Bryan Rothwell (Vicar of Threlkeld, St John's and Wythburn); Jean Scott-Smith and Ted Relph (Lakeland Dialect Society) for their assistance.

GEORGE SMITH (1825 - 1876)
The Skiddaw Hermit

Mary E. Burkett O.B.E.

In 1863 a man of large build and unkempt appearance, about 26 years old, was attracted by the beauties of Keswick from a small place in Aberdeenshire called Pitsligo. At first he took rooms in the town but after a while he started to live rough and became known as the 'Caveman', the 'Skiddaw Hermit' or the 'Dodd Man'. At that time there were many vagrants wandering the country, sometimes doing bits of work or at others merely tramping. The Skiddaw Hermit (or more correctly, the Dodd Man since he built his 'nest' on Dodd, the low fell to the west of Skiddaw) was an individual and a character. His real name was George Smith.

One of eight children, he was born in about 1825 at Crossbrae, Forglen, Banffshire where his father had a croft on the estate of Sir Robert Abercromby as a ground officer. George attended Fordyce School and

Above: The Skiddaw Hermit (detail of 'Main St 1870' by Joseph Brown Jnr.)

Portrait of Mary Graves (private collection)

later Aberdeen University where he had a £16 bursary until poor health forced him to give it up. His mother died when he was a child. His father married again but he too died shortly afterwards and his stepmother was so severe with George that the day after his father's funeral he found himself homeless.

His difficult childhood may account for his wandering life and a lot of his problems. But he was far from being unattractive and had a rich, eloquent and pleasant voice. When in conversation he spoke fast but there was always a most lively expression of concentration on his face. Fred Robinson of Windermere said that 'his eyes reminded you of doves' eyes, they were so gentle, so soft and yet so bright'. He had a good forehead that seemed to show considerable intelligence. Though he lived rough he was initially scrupulously clean and gentlemanly in conversation and manner.

He always carried a staff of about his height and this he grasped a little above the centre.

Soon after he came to the area people noticed that he went from Keswick everyday to Skiddaw and then returned to Keswick each night covered with mud. Eventually they discovered that he had built himself a makeshift 'house' on the slopes of Dodd on a ledge above a cave. There was a small stone wall at the base and then on top a huge frame of rushes and woven saplings, lined with moss and bracken and shaped as a dome or umbrella which could be moved up and down. The whole thing looked so like a nest that G. B. Sticks writing in 1890 described it as 'a great big chitty's nest' or 'a pie' (chitty is a Cumbrian dialect word for a wren). George entered it rather like a wren, from a hole near the top, and evidently made himself very snug as he spent summers and winters living there. He used old sacks or leaves for bedding, and very few people were allowed to visit him: perhaps very few wished to do so since he was compelled to sleep, eat, cook (with tallow in a tin) and live in this little space.

Mr J. Lomax writing in 1956 described him as of middle height and slim, his dark hair standing 'like quills upon the fretful porcupine' and 'he was his own laundress and always washed his one and only wincey shirt in the nearest stream, and dried it on his back'. The hermit used to say 'it's a varra poor back that cud'na dry its ain shirt'. He would walk everywhere barefoot, wearing neither coat nor hat and his trousers were cut off or rolled at the knees. The cover of this book shows a reproduction of a splendid oil painting that hangs in Keswick Museum, called Main Street 1870 by Joseph Brown Junior; it reveals a full-length image of the Hermit standing centre stage surrounded by many worthy residents of the town. He appears barefoot, with a bent stick in one hand and a loaf of bread under his arm. It seems that at that time he was accepted as someone who belonged to the town and was not regarded with disapproval.

Unfortunately George developed a weakness for drink. The Royal Oak was his favourite haunt where he often became senseless with whisky - Glenlivet was his favourite. But how did he manage to earn enough to buy food and fund his drinking? It seems that he earned what he could by painting portraits or making sketches of local people. It became a fashion for local innkeepers and farmers to have their portraits painted by him. He certainly seemed to have an ability to catch likenesses. He was able to produce life-size portraits very quickly and his modest charge of a guinea a time provided his daily needs.

A number of portraits painted by George Smith have been identified, some in private collections, one in Tullie House Museum, and another in Keswick Museum, although this is unlabelled. Some of the finest portraits are two sets of paintings of Tom and Mary Graves of Mirkholme, Bassenthwaite. Family tradition claims that they were painted in return for hospitality given to the Hermit at the farm. None of them is signed or dated, but the earlier pair must date from the mid 1860s and the later from around 1870. Another portrait is of Robert Hebson, originally of Pooley Bridge, who worked as a waiter in a Keswick hotel and used to smuggle out alcohol to the Hermit who in return painted his portrait for nothing - or so the story goes.

When not drunk George could hold intelligent conversation with anyone, and he was well enough liked that people did not consider him a beggar or a cadger. Some of his habits were comic: he used to buy tea and sugar and eat them together, quite dry. When in funds he would buy steak, herring and potatoes, sometimes preferring to eat them raw, even the potatoes.

Apart from painting his other passion was phrenology and physiognomy, both much in vogue at the end of the nineteenth century. At fairs he would claim to tell peoples' characters from feeling the bumps on their heads. Apparently it was quite amazing to hear him describe their characters after meeting them for only a few moments. His character reading formed a popular entertainment for the publicans to provide for the tourists, but he had to put up with some ridicule. He would sometimes preach sermons. Once again people often paid him with his favourite Scotch whisky rendering him paralytically drunk.

Writing in 1890 G. B. Sticks recalled his memories of him thus - 'he spoke the Scottish dialect, his voice was rich and he appeared to be a religious monomaniac'. The Hermit told Mr Sticks that he could not bear to live in a house because he loved nature too much and felt that people should live in the open air to study it all more easily.

As time passed however, it became clear that his popularity in the town was waning. People were put off by his wild appearance and increasingly dirty state. From time to time he had to be put into the police cells, and because he could never pay his fines he was sent to Carlisle jail for a few

Portrait of Robert Hebson (private collection)

weeks. While serving his stint there he evidently painted the governor's portrait. Then eventually a riotous party described as 'roisterous excursionists' wrecked his 'nest' on Dodd and he was drummed out of town leaving a pile of bottles on the fell side. For a while he took refuge on the shores of Windermere near Ambleside and then at Beech Hill, Bowness, where he was often seen in the village. Here he built a small shelter where he lived happily for a time becoming quite an attraction in

Ambleside. But then the drinking bouts began again and it was reported that 'it was like approaching a lion's den to try to come near his tent'. He began using bad language and attacking his visitors physically, so he was ordered away.

The magazine Cumbria of June 1976 (who gleaned it from a contemporary Westmoreland Gazette) records a highly colourful story of a little fracas with the police at Ambleside. He had been accused of creating a riotous disturbance in the street and had failed to turn up at court. Evidently a search party was sent out and he was found in the inn at Troutbeck Bridge. He was about to go quietly until he caught sight of the blue uniformed police. Like a flash he raced off and hid. A renewed search was made, George eluding his pursuers by scaling a wall. Eventually they led him quietly back to court and after an extraordinarily long performance he was given seven days - it seems that his offences were treated mildly considering the diversions they had caused.

He then walked to Holburn Hill at Millom where Mrs Beetham reformed him temporarily at her hotel. Eventually he was chased to Barrow; perhaps he was becoming ill and was certainly more unstable than before. It is said that he mended his ways after hearing a preacher at an open air service at Windermere. The preacher came from Seacombe near Liverpool and after listening to him George was converted to Christianity. Apparently he began wearing more conventional clothes, reformed his habits and even gave up drinking. He decided he wanted to buy a bible, selected one and paid for it. He laid it down flat upon its side, took up a knife and cut off half the back. Amid the protestations of those who were watching he then turned it onto its other side and cut off the rest of the back. Taking up the book and holding it in his hand he said, 'This is to show you that henceforth this word of God must be an open book to me: it has been a closed book long enough'.

Early photographs of the preacher's services showed the Dodd Man always in attendance listening at the edge of the crowd. Many of the drawings published in the articles written about him at the time are copies of photographs taken by Moses Bowness from Ambleside and a Mr Whittaker of Penrith. Whatever truth there is in the story of his conversion it did not keep him in Cumbria for in about 1873 he returned to Scotland. He died of 'inflammation of the brain' in the Banffshire Lunatic Asylum on 28th September 1876.

It cannot be claimed that George Smith was Keswick's most famous or talented artist but he was certainly one of the most colourful. The last members of what was known as the Cockermouth School were much more proficient and better qualified, but George's price of a guinea a head may have been more attractive! His likenesses were supposedly marvellous, his technique simple, the poses direct and uncomplicated, and backgrounds usually plain. They showed characteristic features of the farming community in which he had lived and which he admired. The faces are of kindly and gentle people who show the marks of hard work in a rugged climate. Despite his artistic simplicity his talent was sought after, and as a local character the Skiddaw Hermit certainly deserves a place in the history of Keswick.

Note: this chapter is adapted from M.E.Burkett: *The Skiddaw Hermit*, 1996 Skiddaw Press.

Further reading:
Information about George Smith's life is very fragmentary and largely anecdotal - for example:
G. B. Sticks: *North Country Lore & Legend*, 1890
Cumbrian Letterbox, Cumbria vol. 6, no. 6, 1956
Cumbrian Letterbox, Cumbria June 1976
Cumberland News, July 30th 1982 *The Cadging Caveman who nested on Skiddaw Dodd.*

JAMES CLIFTON WARD (1843 - 1880)
A man of science and of god

Alan Smith

Many of the Keswick characters in this book were Cumbrian born and in their various ways became 'local heroes'. Clifton Ward was the welcome outsider. Posted to Keswick by his employers, a place not of his own choosing, he nevertheless quickly made his mark, and within a few years, had become a pillar of the local community. His energetic involvement in many aspects of Keswick life and his driving force to get things done, endeared him to many in the town. The legacy of his work and life in Keswick lives on today. His life was tragically short, but active and influential.

He was born on the 13th April 1843 at Clapham in South London, the son of James Ward, a schoolmaster, and Mary Ann Ward. It appears his

Above: James Clifton Ward (Date unknown, but probably circa 1870). Reproduced with permission from British Geological Survey.

health was always delicate and, as a result, he was sent to school at Hastings in the hope that the bracing Sussex air would help him. For long periods he was taken out of school and given free rein for an outdoor life on the South Downs. It was here that he learnt the joys of observing natural history. He went back to London in 1861 and entered the Royal School of Mines as a student of the then burgeoning subject of geology. He was a successful student, gaining the prestigious Edward Forbes Medal in 1864. Ill health continued to trouble him and consequently he never graduated, but was granted the Associateship of the Royal School of Mines (a degree equivalent qualification). In 1865, at the age of 22 he was appointed to the Geological Survey of England and Wales and was almost immediately sent to the West Riding of Yorkshire to survey the millstone grit rocks of the Pennines. In 1868 he was transferred to the Lake District and was based in Keswick.

In 1868 the Geological Survey of England and Wales was in its infancy, but its purpose was to begin to survey and compile maps of the rocks of the country and assess its mineral resources. The spur to this work had been the completion of the first Ordnance Survey maps, providing accurate and detailed topographical maps of the country for the first time. The new six inch to one mile scale maps (1:10,560) for Keswick and the Lake District were finished in the early 1860s. As a departure from the previous practice of being London based, the Survey had decided to post its surveyors out into the provinces.

Ward's task was to carry out the first professional mapping of Quarter Sheet 101 SE, covering over 200 square miles of the northern Lake District. It stretched from Ennerdale in the west, to Ullswater in the east and included the high fells from Great Gable and Helvellyn to Skiddaw and Blencathra. This was a very formidable task; a tough piece of country, virtually unknown geologically. For a young, relatively inexperienced geologist it was great challenge. Ward had probably never seen before many of the kinds of rocks he came across around Keswick, although we do know he had been to Italy and had been enthralled by some of the volcanic rocks he witnessed on Vesuvius and in the area around Naples. Perhaps this was one of the reasons why he was chosen to come to Keswick, for it was known at the time that many of the rocks of the area were of volcanic origin. The regulations of the time for officers of the Survey specified 9 hours of work per day, for 6 days a week, with a salary

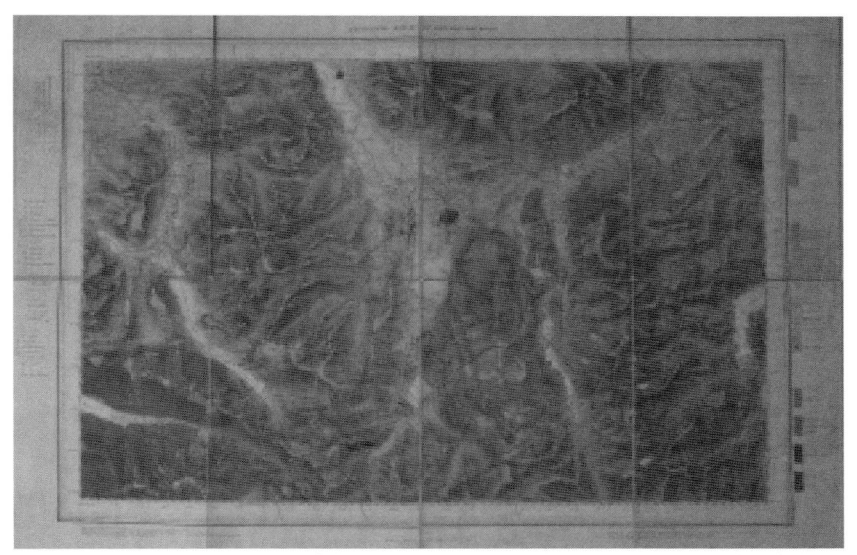

Ward's Map (published folded at the one inch to one mile scale, fully coloured 1875).

of £2 1s per week (probably a comfortable amount in those days). The 1871 census returns show him as an unmarried boarder living in High Street (house not specified). It is interesting to picture Ward's life, tramping the fells, day in, day out, in all weathers, with his maps, notebook, and hammer, collecting and identifying rocks, fossils and minerals, carefully recording them and painstakingly working out the geology of the area. He had completed his mapping by 1875. In December of that year the Survey published his work, a fine, engraved, full coloured map of the area, available in flat or fine linen folded format at the popular one inch to one mile scale. This map remained the only official Geological Survey map of the Keswick area for 123 years. In 1876 Ward's explanatory Memoir to accompany the map, *The Geology of the Northern Part of the English Lake District* was published and marked the end of his project in Keswick. Both map and Memoir are now collector's items. This was undoubtedly an outstanding piece of work. It is also very clear Ward did this single-handed. Although he was technically 'under the superintendence' of the district surveyor, a more senior geologist by the name of W. T. Aveline, examination of his field note books that had to be deposited

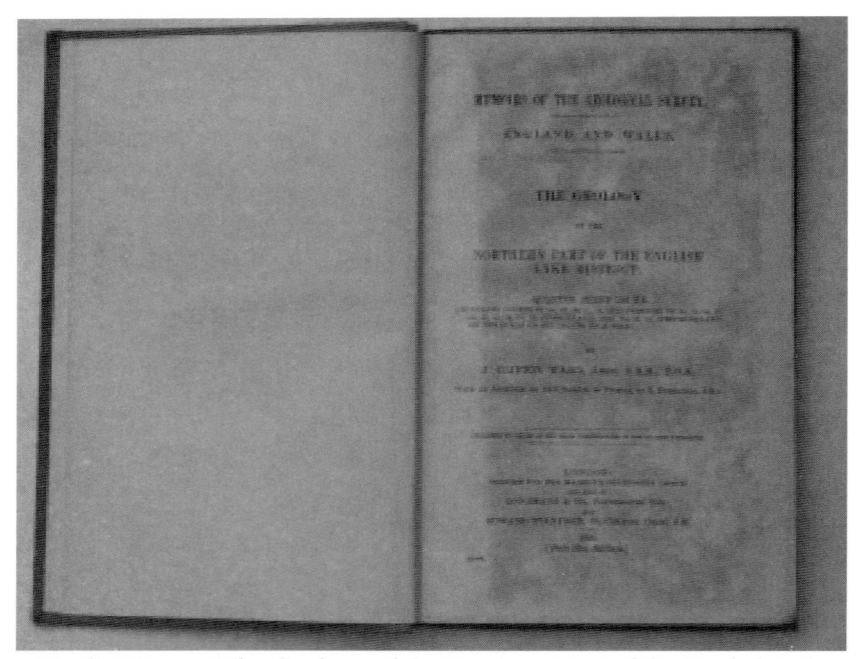

Ward's Memoir 'The Geology of the Northern Part of the English Lake District 1876.

with the Survey (now in the British Geological Survey archives at Keyworth, Nottingham) reveals the work was Ward's alone.

Ward should be remembered for this significant piece of professional geological work alone. This is not the place to probe the detail of the work, nor to compare his interpretations of the rocks in the 1870s with those of today, but it salutary that when the current British Geological Survey came to remap in modern terms the same area covered by Ward, it was done by a team of 19 geologists, taking 17 years from 1982 to 1999, as compared with a little over six years by Ward alone. He mapped the outcrop patterns of the local rocks extremely accurately and his work stands up very well when compared with the present modern maps. He had been trained at the Royal School of Mines in the then comparatively new technique of looking at rocks in thin section down a microscope; his work in the Lakes was one of the first regional surveys to use that method to advantage. It was Ward who first looked at the volcanic rocks of the area, applying his knowledge of what he had seen on Vesuvius. He coined the name 'Borrowdale Volcanic Series' for these rocks in the Keswick area, a term still recognised worldwide today in geological circles. Ward was also the first person to describe some of the features of the glacial history of the area. It is fascinating today to read his accounts, for even as late as the 1870s the idea that ice once existed on land and could be an erosional force was still not totally accepted, many proponents of 'the biblical flood' were still invoking inundations by the sea up to great heights.. Ward himself still erred towards this belief. His notebooks show he conversed a great deal with local people particularly about the mines and mineral deposits of the area. There are many references to conversations with a Mr Crosthwaite and Captain Francis. Some of Ward's original six inch to one mile field maps are in the Keswick Museum, along with many of his geological specimens and some fine plaster geological models of the landscape which Ward also found time to make.

Ward's work for the Survey established his national reputation, but in Keswick here was a man who also devoted his seemingly boundless energy to an amazing range of other activities and organisations. He was a prolific writer and lecturer, not just on geological topics. During his short stay in Yorkshire before coming to Keswick he produced an elementary school book on physics. During his Keswick years he repeated a similar exercise for geology, the text being essentially nine talks he first delivered to schoolchildren and as public lectures in Keswick. In addition to that, between 1870 and 1879 he wrote no less than 22 papers in a variety of scientific and geological journals, all essentially stemming from his Survey work and developing his ideas on Lakeland rocks and landscape.

The character and dynamism of the man is best exemplified by the ways he adopted to popularise science, and geology in particular, in Keswick and the Lakeland society of the day. Close to his time of arrival in the Lake District the Keswick Literary Society had been founded. His name was not on the original list of members in 1869, but in the second session in 1870 he gave a lecture on 'The Geological History of Italy'. From that point on, his name appears frequently in the Society minutes. In 1872 he spoke on 'Some low forms of life and their connection with Geology'. In the same year he proposed the Society should become the Keswick Literary and Scientific Society which it eventually did in 1874, with (no surprise) James Clifton Ward as its President in 1874, 1875 and 1876. The Society still exists today as the Keswick Lecture Society and has currently just completed its 136th Season. Ward's name appeared frequently in the list of speakers and it is remarkable the range of topics he was able to speak upon. In 1873 he lectured on 'The Old Glaciers of Borrowdale'. In 1874 he spoke on 'The Ear, its structure and Development', in 1876 on 'Electrochemical Decomposition' and 'Some Analogies between Sound and Light - experimentally illustrated', and then in 1877 on ' The Life of Faraday '.

In June 1873 he instigated geological field trips for the Society into the local area and the press reports in the West Cumberland Times of the day make fascinating reading of Ward's irrepressible leadership. They paint evocative pictures of Victorian life; for example in 1873, 170 people went to Borrowdale where 'the grass fields of the How at Rosthwaite provided a convenient auditorium for Mr Ward to describe the Geological History of Borrowdale'. In 1874 on a trip to Greenside Mine, Glenridding, he led a large section of the party, first over Sticks Pass on foot, where 'the inquisitive hammer was in constant requisition to enquire within' and then on to the Glenridding Hotel for a lavish Cumberland tea.. Or, in 1875, 'Mr J.C. Ward took twenty men and nine women in three waggonettes to Seathwaite and on foot 'by easy stages' to the summit of Sca Fell Pike. There were still large patches of snow and ice in Piers Ghyll and, needless to say, Mr Ward took the opportunity of making remarks at suitable places upon the geological features of the district'. There was an excursion to examine the remarkable boulders measuring 17 x 14 feet behind Lyzzick Hall. In May 1875 they had an excursion to Crummock Water looking at the glacially smoothed rocks on the shore ....and 'Mr Ward sounded the depth of the lake off Mellbreak'. 1876 saw an excursion to Grasmere, up to Easedale Tarn, and then...'some of the ladies rowed across Codale Tarn'.

One of Ward's most valuable contributions to scientific life was the setting up of the Cumberland and Westmorland Association for the Advancement of Literature and Science in 1875. This was done at Ward's instigation. He became its first Secretary, Treasurer and Editor in 1875. The published Transactions of the Society became a significant record of local scientific research for many years. It embraced groups in Carlisle, Maryport, Longtown, Silloth and Ambleside as well as in Keswick. Unfortunately it has not survived.

There is a minute in the records of the Keswick Literary and Scientific Society dated 31st March 1873 resolving that Mr Clifton Ward, Canon Battersby and Dr Knight should 'take steps to found a Museum in Keswick'. Meetings took place in the Library (now the Battersby Hall) and collections of various kinds began to be assembled. Interestingly, on the first field excursion of the society in the 1873 season, after Ward had conducted a group around Grange, the Bowder Stone and Rosthwaite, tea was provided at the Borrowdale Hotel at 5.30 pm, after which 'the newly formed Museum Committee gave an interim report'. Ward immediately became responsible for the rock and mineral collections and he appears to have been appointed hon. curator around about the same time. When he retired from this post in March 1877 after a term of office ' signalised by indefatigable efforts to promote scientific knowledge' it is recorded the collection in the Library consisted of 286 birds eggs, 402 zoological exhibits, 1327 geological specimens and 64 antiquities. Ward used this Library base for some of his public talks. Typically he used specimens as visual aids. In his talk on the 'Old Volcanoes of Cumberland' in January 1875 it is reported he had hand specimens of rocks from Vesuvius and the Lake District...and 'even the practised eye could not distinguish between them'. He had a large geological map measuring 12 x 9 feet, numerous coloured diagrams and 7 microscopes with rocks in thin section.

Ward's field note books in the British Geological Survey archives at Keyworth, Nottingham, help to give an insight into the man, his approach to fieldwork and of the way he conducted his work. It is clear he conversed with local people a great deal. The books contain large numbers of field sketches - some merely aide-memoires in pencil, others very neat, precise pen and ink sketches. He seems to have liked to put his thoughts on paper - laying out his analysis of problems, giving the theoretical background and field evidence for his opinions. Most interesting of all is his propensity to write in verse, often expressing a deep religious outlook on things and an almost mythical philosophy. A classic example is three pages of verse running to 19 stanzas which are recorded simply as 'afternoon walk - 9/8/71 '. Quoting just one typical stanza of this:

> *The flowers that by the wayside grow*
> *The insect, bird and creeping things,*
> *Wood, rock and everlasting hills*
> *All glory to their God do bring.*

it is clear that underpinning all his thoughts were deep religious convictions.

Between all this activity of working six days a week as a field geologist, writing scientific papers, lecturing, assembling a museum collection, being President, Secretary and Treasurer of various societies, he found time to get married in 1877. His bride was Elizabeth Ann Benson, the daughter of a Cockermouth solicitor, Robert Benson. On his return to Keswick after his honeymoon, in February 1877 the Keswick Literary and Scientific Society made a presentation to Ward and his wife at a special gathering ... of 'an oak chest containing a silver tea pot, coffee pot, sugar basin and cream jug, each article engraved on it the interlaced monograms of Mr and Mrs Ward. The design is that known as the Indian pattern and it excited general admiration'. Canon Battersby in his presentation speech said .... 'for a long time, there had been a strong feeling in Keswick at least some acknowledgement was due to Mr. J. Clifton Ward for the great assiduity, earnestness and devotion which he had displayed in the interest of the Society and also for the advancement of science in the town.(applause)' The Wards had two daughters, born in the first years of their marriage.

Ward's work with the Geological Survey in Keswick was completed in 1877 with the publication of the Memoir. For a short time he was transferred to the Carlisle area and worked around the Bewcastle district. There is some indication that his health was not good in 1876-7 and that he was seeking a less physically exhausting job than a field geologist. Throughout his life he had held deep religious beliefs. The next biographical record of him was his ordination into the Church of England at Carlisle Cathedral in 1878. He gave up his position with the Survey in 1877 and appropriately came back to Keswick as assistant curate at St John's Church. In Slater's Directory of 1879 the Wards are recorded as living in Blencathra Street (no number is given, but, in view of the date, this was probably a newly built house at the Southey Street end) He stayed in this post for just over a year, but there is little record of his work. In 1880 he was appointed perpetual curate at Rydal in south Lakeland. Within a few weeks of taking up the post he caught a chill and died on the 16th April at the age of 37.

Tributes to him were lavish. The Cumberland and Westmorland Association raised money to mount a tablet to his memory, with £300 surplus money going to assist with the education of his two young daughters. Fittingly he was brought back to be buried in the graveyard at St John's, Keswick. The memorial tablet erected on the south wall in the church praising his contribution to geology and life in Keswick is still to be seen today.

Canon Rawnsley wrote a sonnet to his honour for his funeral. This was a fitting tribute to an indefatigable man.

The Geologist's Funeral

Bury him here, and let his body's dust
Be ash to ash in this volcanic land
Whose fiery secrets he could understand
Right well may we his dissolution trust
To that same Will that through the lava crust
Spouted the granite fountains God! whose hand
Of this earth's waste new continents hath planned,
Into thy potter's clay a gem we thrust.
No more his feet we follow up the cleft,
Or hear his questioning hammer tap and ring,
And learn which way the primal bergs were rolled;
But till the Greta ceases sorrowing,
We leave him here, contented to be left,
Schooled in a lore whose days are aeons old.

Further reading.
There are few written accounts of Ward, other than obituary notices and a short entry in the *Dictionary of National Biography*. For an account and evaluation of his geological work and a full listing of his writings see Alan Smith: *James Clifton Ward (1843-1880) An Early Populariser of Geology* in *The Rock Men: Pioneers of Lakeland Geology*. Cumberland Geological Society, pp 75-81, 2001.

HARDWICKE DRUMMOND RAWNSLEY (1851 - 1920)
'The most active volcano in Europe'

Alan Hankinson

In every field of British activity the Victorian period produced men of high confidence and incredible vitality. They operated at the top levels of excellence, often in different levels of endeavour at once, always tirelessly. In these more effete times, it is enough to make one feel exhausted just to read about their lives and all the things they managed to do - men like John Ruskin (artist and critic, lecturer and social prophet) and Mr Gladstone (statesman, scholar, orator) and the novelist Charles Dickens. There were dozens more like them, men who hurled themselves at life's challenges and never seemed to run out of steam. The outstanding example in Cumbria and the Lake District was Canon Hardwicke Drummond Rawnsley. One of his Keswick parishioners described him as "the most active volcano in Europe".

Grevel Lindop in his masterly Literary Guide to the Lake District sums up Rawnsley's accomplishments in these words: "….. minor poet, disciple of Ruskin, patron of arts and handicrafts, conservationist, fighter for public access to the countryside, biographer, topographer and local historian, placer of monuments and inscriptions, indefatigable lecturer, joint founder of the National Trust, a generous, devout and socially-concerned clergyman who seems to have enjoyed every moment of his incredibly full life".

Rawnsley was a Lake District man by adoption, not by origin or upbringing. His family were old-established Lincolnshire folk, mostly clergymen, and he grew up at first on the banks of the Thames, then at Halton Holgate in Lincolnshire, where his father was rector and the Tennysons were near-neighbours and close friends. He went to Uppingham School where the head-master Edward Thring introduced him to the poetry of Wordsworth. The young Rawnsley immediately became a compulsive poet himself and spent several summer holidays exploring the vales and fells around Grasmere.

He went to Oxford, more to distinguish himself as an athlete than a scholar, though he took degrees first in Classics, then in Natural Science. The great Oxford influence on him, though, was that of the Slade Professor of Fine Arts, John Ruskin, then at the height of his prodigious powers and fame as lecturer, teacher and inspirational figure. Rawnsley was one of the undergraduates – Oscar Wilde, amazingly, was another – who risked the jeers and sneers of their contemporaries by going out to Hinksey to work on Ruskin's road improvement scheme there.

There was never much doubt that Rawnsley was going to be an Anglican cleric. It was the family tradition and it accorded naturally with his fervent, pious and beneficent spirit. He had a compelling urge to out into the outside world and do good. He was sent to a very rough part of Bristol to try missionary work, and found it hard. By his own account, he was "half parson, half policeman". But it was here, in 1877, that he published the first of nearly forty books – A Book of Bristol Sonnets – and it was here, too, that he inaugurated his life-long career as a public campaigner. He fought to save an ancient church tower from destruction and, as so often in later years, he won.

He was ordained a priest at Carlisle Cathedral in 1877 at the age of twenty-six, and sent to take up the living at Wray on the western side of Lake Windermere. He assumed his duties – preaching, pastoral, social –

with the enthusiasm that he took to everything. He set up classes in wood-carving and launched a series of campaigns to stop greedy developers from destroying the special quality of Lake District life and landscape. There was a scheme to build a railway alongside Derwentwater and up Borrowdale to the summit of Honister Pass to transport slate from the quarry there to Keswick. There was a scheme to push a railway into Ennerdale. There were plans to extend the line from Windermere to Ambleside. Rawnsley organised the protesting pressure groups, and did the bulk of the work himself, and prevailed in every case. He created the Lake District Defence Society. He was a formidable force and made, not surprisingly, many enemies. One man, who had worked for him as gardener, said he was "a peppery old devil". But he was effective and in those days, long before the formation of the Friends of the Lake District, there was an urgent need for such a tenacious and skilful defender of the District.

It was during these first pastoral days at Wray that he met and made friends with some rich visitors from London, Mr Rupert Potter and his family, who had rented Wray Castle for their summer holidays. He made particular friends with the dutiful daughter, Beatrix. He shared her interest in botany and was the first published author she had ever met. Nearly twenty years later she showed him a story she had written to amuse some children she knew and he was impressed by her work and her illustrations, and encouraged her to publish. The little book was The Tale of Peter Rabbit, an immediate success and the first of many such stories that have an evergreen appeal to children. It was the money she earned from these publications that enabled Miss Potter to transform her life and become, vary happily, a Lakeland sheep farmer. She did not forget her debt to Canon Rawnsley.

In the summer of 1883 he transferred to the living of Crosthwaite, Keswick's parish church, and he and his wife Edith moved into the old vicarage, their home and the centre of their work for the next thirty-four years. The house still stands, on a superb hill-top site that commands fine southward views to Derwentwater and the Newlands fells. The poet Thomas Gray had stayed there in October 1769, on his seminal trip to the Lake District, and had written to a friend: "I got to the Parsonage a little before sunset and saw in my glass a picture, that if I could transmit it to you, and fix it in all the softness of its living colours, would fairly sell for

Hardwicke and Beatrix Potter at Windermere, 1912

a thousand pounds. This is the sweetest scene I can yet discover in point of pastoral beauty; the rest are in a sublimer style". Rawnsley had these words incised into a slab of stone, which he set into the terrace wall at the top of the handsome, sloping garden.

His first step was to establish a parish magazine, in the first issue of which he gave this promise to his new flock: "I shall come to Crosthwaite not only as an ecclesiastic and Church official, not only as a minister and superintendent of the religious services in church, mission room and Sunday school ..... I shall come as one who holds himself pledged to encourage all good work, and who will try – God helping him - to preach that best of sermons among his friends and fellows – the life of Christian justice, temperance, tolerance and charity".

It is a true statement of his creed. He lived at a time when many Anglican priests tortured themselves continually with doctrinal doubts and difficulties, submitting themselves and those around them to hours of angst about whether they stood in the right part of the wide Christian spectrum. Rawnsley had no such troubles. His faith was simple, direct and practical, based on the words of Jesus. If he ever suffered doubts, he did not display them. He looked after his own family, cared for his parishioners, and in local and national affairs of many kinds he fought the good fight with courage and cheerful persistence and great industry.

When local, landowners, on Latrigg and at Fawe Park, blocked off ancient rights-of-way, he organised mass demonstrations and forced the removal of the barriers. He campaigned hard against the idea of a railway to the summit of Snowden, one of the few fights that he lost. In 1900 he ran the campaign of protest against a plan to establish an electric tram-way between Bowness and Ambleside, and this one he won.

Perhaps the most important of his achievements, certainly the one for which he is chiefly remembered today, was the formation of the National Trust. It was in 1893, when the land around Lodore Falls and the island of Grasmere were both up for sale, that he launched the notion that such places should be public property and carefully conserved. He talked it over with an old friend, the philanthropist Octavia Hill, and a legal expert, Sir Robert Hunter, and soon the National Trust for Places of Historic Interest and Natural Beauty was established, with Rawnsley as Secretary. He remained its Secretary – and its dynamo – until the end of his life.

It was he, in 1902, who raised £6500 in five months to purchase Brandlehow Woods below Catbells, the Trust's first property in the Lake District, to allow public access to the shores of Derwentwater. Four years later he raised £12800 to acquire 750 acres of Gowbarrow Fell above Ullswater. The ball was well and truly rolling, and has gone on rolling ever since so that more than a century after its foundation in 1895 the National Trust owns and safeguards more than a quarter of the Lake District. Always happy to transpose his thoughts into a few lines of verse, sometimes serious, sometimes light, he wrote: "I came and preached until I bust, the sacred name of the National Trust".

All the time he was writing – letters and sermons, lectures and articles, occasional poems and countless sonnets. To the modern reader, the sonnets are the great stumbling block. There are thousands of them, all of them serous and high-minded, each of them carefully crafted, every single one of them, as far as my researches go – dull and lifeless. He was attempting the Wordsworth note and he simply could not do it. His prose writings, too, are frequently uninspired – long descriptive pieces about Lakeland vistas and sunsets, couched in a self-conscious "poetical" language and often spilling over into the mushy sentimentalism that the Victorian readers could take. But he had a clear, flowing, undemanding style, and when he was dealing with Cumbrian history, and local folk-lore, and the literary associations of the Lake District, he could be informative and entertaining. His masterpiece, in my view, is an article he wrote to be read to the annual meeting of the Wordsworth Society in 1882, which he entitled "Reminiscences of Wordsworth Among the Peasantry of Westmorland".

He had the bright idea, when he was still a young vicar at Wray, of seeking out the old folk of the Grasmere and Rydal area who had memories of Wordsworth and getting them to tell their tales. It is a funny, fascinating and revealing report, invaluable in the sense that had Rawnsley not done the research when he did the information he gathered would have been lost for ever. He had a sharp ear and quickly mastered the art of reproducing the local dialect sounds, in speech and ion the page. He also had the art of getting people to speak frankly, and their recollections and assessments of "Wadsworth", as they all called him, are vivid and surprising. None of them read his poetry or rated it at all. Most of them much preferred that of Hartley Coleridge, and some believed that Hartley really wrote the poems for which Wordsworth had been given all the credit. Others thought Dorothy Wordsworth had written the poems. But many recalled the old poet walking the valley lanes, speaking to no one, but mumbling noisily to himself as he went along, trying out the lines he was working on and frightening the local children. He was stiff and stand-offish – "not a man as could crack wi' fwoakes" – and one old man, who had delivered butter to Rydal Mount as a lad, delivered this terrible judgement: "a desolate-minded man, ye kna ….. It was potry as did it ….. his hobby, ye mun kna, was potry. It was a queer thing, but it would like eneuf cause him to be desolate …..".

Soon after they moved to Keswick it occurred to Rawnsley and his wife that there was a need for some form of useful occupation that would help keep the working men and boys town out of the pubs on the long winter evenings. Rawnsley was a dedicated teetotaller, always on the lookout for positive ways of distracting his weaker brethren from the temptations of the demon drink. So they started evening classes, three nights a week in the parish rooms, giving instruction in painting and woodcarving and metal work. It was part of the Ruskin message, the need to keep alive the traditional craftsmen's skills, to preserve the dignity of labour in the teeth of the ever-encroaching factory system of machine-minders. It was a great success. After four years, their classes had nearly seventy regular attendants. So they decided they needed their own building, raised the money, and, in 1894, opened the Keswick School of Industrial Arts. It flourished until 1894, when it was transformed into La Primavera, an Italian restaurant.

For seven years Rawnsley served on Cumberland County Council, campaigning vigorously for footpath preservation, proper signposts and public health measures. He was particularly concerned over tuberculosis which was a great scourge in those days, fighting for strict controls mover the purity of milk supplies and organising the setting up of the sanatorium above Threlkeld. Later in life he was a ferocious campaigner against the new fashion for white-bleached bread, which he denounced so roundly that he was threatened with an action for libel.

Animal welfare was another of his causes. He fought against visection, rabbit coursing, and the mass slaughter of birds for their plumage.

He fought, too, against the rising flood of dirty novels, magazines and photographs and vulgar seaside postcards which, he proclaimed, were "poisoning the nation's character at its fountain-head", in other words, by corrupting its young. It often seems as if Rawnsley's influence was negative – preventing developments in the Lake District, urging the suppression of pornography. He certainly wanted these measures taken, but he knew the importance of being positive as well. So he pressed for properly-run, free public libraries and worked hard to improve education, especially at Keswick School. In 1907 he formed the Secondary School Association, and acted as its secretary until his death. And he was an ambitious celebrator. It was he, in 1885, who launched the May Queen procession and festivities in Keswick, which the town no longer celebrates. And he loved bonfires. On June 22nd, 1887 he presided over the bonfire on the summit of Skiddaw to mark the Queen's Golden Jubilee. Ten years later, for her Diamond Jubilee, he organised 2584 bonfires across Great Britain. It is said that from the summit of Skidded he was able to see 148 of his other bonfires cheerfully blazing.

He was a compulsive commemorator too, always ready to arrange for an inscribed stone to mark some significant piece of local history. In 1881 he saw to the setting up of the Brothers' Parting Stone, marking the point where William Wordsworth said goodbye to his sailor brother John at the top of Grisdale Pass. When Ruskin died in 1900, Rawnsley organised the monument on Friar's Crag. There were many more, and it is entirely appropriate that Rawnsley should have his own tributary stone alongside the path between Friar's Crag and Keswick boat-landings.

It is not surprising that, in the midst of all this activity, he should suffer occasional breakdowns in health, brought about by over-work. His solution was to take long trips abroad – the Holy Land, the Alps, Greece and Italy, the United States – and when he returned home, fully recovered, he would give lectures about his experiences.

In 1893 he was appointed an honorary canon of Carlisle Cathedral. A few years later he was offered the Bishopric of Madagascar but, after long thought, he gave way to the importuning of many friends and opted to stay in Keswick.

His wife Edith died in 1916 and Rawnsley retired a few months later, to live at Allan Bank – the Wordsworths' old home in Grasmere. He remarried in 1918 and continued to keep himself busy – designing war memorials, organising bonfires to celebrate peace, until his death in May 1920. He left Allan Bank, of course, to the National Trust.

Just over twenty years later the Trust received another and much greater bequest. In her will Beatrix Potter, remembering her old debt to Canon Rawnsley, left more than four thousand acres of fell farmland and many hundreds of Herdwick sheep.

It is hard to think of anyone, at any time, who had a more powerful influence over Lake District affairs of all kinds than Hardwicke Drummond Rawnsley, an influence that was almost entirely beneficial. There ought to be full-length, fully documented biography of him. But there is not, nothing more than a brief, uncritical account of his life by his second wife Eleanor that was published in 1923. Several writers have proposed a biography, but no publisher has warmed to the idea. Well, publishers are like that. But Canon Rawnsley was a persistent man, and his memory is persistent too, and his time will surely come …..

Alan Hankinson 2006
Previously published in 'Cumbria Life'.

Further reading:
Brian Wilkinson: *The Rawnsley Trail*, Bookcase, 2006.

JOHN TOMLINSON (TOM) WILSON (1887 - 1961)
'T' PUP chap'

Brian Wilkinson

Many house names in the Lake District town of Keswick reflect the names of the surrounding mountains, lakes or locations which are special to the house owner. But one semi-detached house on High Hill bears a name that appears vaguely Asiatic. The house name is 'Maymyo'.

'Maymyo' on High Hill, Keswick

The country formerly known as Burma is now Myanmar. Maymyo is a 'hill station' 67 kilometres east of Mandalay in the Shan Hills. The town ('Maytown'), was named by a British officer, Colonel May of the 5th Bengal Infantry Regiment, who commanded a Battalion of British soldiers there. The town has many English features, including the Purcell Clock Tower presented by Queen Victoria, chiming on the hour to the tune of Big Ben and the Botanical Gardens built during the First World War by Turkish prisoners.

'Maymyo' was the home in Keswick until his death at the age of 74 years of John Tomlinson Wilson, known to all as Tom Wilson, 'T' PUP Chap'. He was born and bred in the town and became well known for his charity work, his allegiance to his old school and the church at Crosthwaite, his articles in The Keswick Reminder in Cumbrian dialect and the several guide books he wrote - with a pleasing turn of phrase and wry humour. Throughout his life Tom Wilson busied himself doing good works for the benefit of both 'locals' and visitors.

Tom was a founder member of the PUPs - 'The Pushing Young People's Society'.

According to reports in the PUPs Annuals of 1934 and 1935, the total funds raised by the PUPs since 1929 was £641. No doubt this figure was exceeded in the following years. £641 in 1932 would be the equivalent of nearly £30,000 in 2006. In 1929 £80 was given to the Town Publicity

Association, when it was in danger of being wound up through lack of support and money; in 1930 £260 was donated for the construction of a shelter in the Park (which is still standing), and represented at the time the cost of building a of a 'good house'; in 1931 twelve seats were placed 'in good positions' in the town; in 1932 £100 was given for the purchase of a the clock for the Council Chambers; in 1933 a further donation of £40 was made to the Publicity Association and in 1934 £161 was given towards the extension of the Cumberland Infirmary at Carlisle. Amongst later gifts to the town was a silver and enamelled chain of office for the Chairman of the Urban District Council, made at the Keswick School of Industrial Arts. The PUPs aimed to provide for Keswick 'those things that were not provided by anyone else'.

How did a local man come to name his house after a small town, a colonial hill station in Burma? The first world war disrupted the lives of many men born in the later years of the nineteenth century and changed the whole face of society. Many young men from Keswick died in Flanders, as the war memorial at County Corner testifies, but others spent the war years in locations where they were fortunate enough to experience little actual battle, posted to the outposts of what was then the British Empire. Tom Wilson was one of these men, a member of the 4th Battalion of the Border Regiment, one of the Regiment's two pre-war Territorial Force Battalions, whose soldiers were all local men recruited from Carlisle and district, east Cumberland, Brampton, Penrith, Keswick and the whole of Westmorland.

At the beginning of the first world war the servicemen were all volunteers, urged to join the army by Lord Kitchener - 'Your Country Needs You' - and encouraged by pressure from the public.

Tom's service life began at the age of twenty-seven years with mobilisation of the 4th Battalion of the Border Regiment in August 1914. He and his companions travelled to Carlisle, and then on to Walney Island at Barrow in Furness. They were joined by men from Kendal. Tom became close friends with several of the Kendal men, one of whom also eventually named his house in Milnthorpe 'Maymyo'. It was presumed that there would be some further training taking place which the men would continue in Sittingbourne, Kent, where the battalion arrived in September. Towards the end of September Lord Kitchener decided to send three divisions of Territorials to India to replace the regular troops which were

4th Battalion, The Border Regiment (Tom Wilson front row, left and Lieutenant Percy M Hope sixth from left third row from the rear)

needed to fight in Europe. There was a promise that at the end of six months they would return. The Territorials were told that they 'would have all the honours of the war just as if they had gone to France'.

At the end of October the Territorials sailed from Southampton for Bombay in HMS Deseado and arrived in Rangoon early in December to relieve the 1st Battalion of the Border regiment. One of the officers was Lieutenant Percy Mirehouse Hope from Keswick, an architect, whom Tom knew quite well.

The Battalion arrived in Maymyo and moved into their quarters, which had until recently been occupied by the 1st Battalion the Border Regiment, a regular battalion which had just returned to England. Somewhere in India the two trains carrying the 4th and the 1st Battalions passed each other, the 4th heading east and the 1st's heading west; sadly many of those serving with the 1st Battalion would not survive until the end of the war.

Soon several members of the Battalion were sent to Mandalay where the tribes who lived in the Kachin Hills had become 'troublesome' and perhaps Tom, with other members of the Battalion, were members of the 'small punitive expeditionary force' sent to move about the troubled area. That would have been Tom's first experience of war action. But there were reminders of home in Burma. During his time in Mandalay Tom saw a large mural of Ashness Bridge above an arch in the Museum there, the largest reproduction of the picture ever made by the Abraham Brothers in Keswick and he remembered finding railway lines marked 'the Workington Iron and Steel Company'.

Tom was eventually promoted to Brigade Signals Sergeant and perhaps included in his duties was the supervision of those Turkish prisoners building the Botanical Gardens which still survive in Maymyo.

The Battalion remained in Burma until early 1918 when it was relieved and transferred to Jubbulpore in India. The war had ended and the Battalion left Peshawar in November 1919 to sail to Plymouth on Her Majesty's Troopship Friedrichsruh.

The Territorials travelled by train first to Kendal and then to Carlisle, where they were demobilised on 31st January 1920.

For men who had probably never travelled far in their own country Burma must have been a revelation - and sufficiently impressed Tom to name his eventual home in Keswick after the small Burmese town where he spent his war years.

And so ended Tom's long but fairly uneventful war. During his service abroad, Tom had helped to provide entertainment for the troops by organising concert parties. His talents as a producer were to be developed in Keswick with the dramatic and musical societies and particularly the Keswick Amateur Operatic and Dramatic Society, presenting musical shows in the town's 'Queen of the Lakes Pavilion'. Tom was the producer of the shows, which included 'New Moon', 'The Vagabond King', 'The Desert Song' and 'Les Cloches de Corneville' - very popular in the nineteen-twenties and thirties, but rarely performed today.

Tom and the other Keswick men came home to Keswick. He resumed working for the family business next to the Post Office and Lieutenant Hope, now Colonel Hope, returned to his architectural firm in Station Street.

John Tomlinson Wilson, known to all as 'Tom' Wilson, was born in a house in Tithebarn Street, Keswick, now demolished, on 5th January 1887. He regarded himself as 'Keswick's first Jubilee baby' - Queen Victoria's Jubilee celebration was celebrated in 1887. Tom's father, John Harrison Wilson, was born in Keswick but his paternal grandfather had come to Keswick from the north east to work on the new railway line being constructed - the Cockermouth, Keswick and Penrith Railway. He

Crosthwaite Free School and Church (pen and ink drawing by Tom Wilson from a painting by W. Westall, 1818)

was a whitesmith (a craftsman who works with tin rather than iron) who had been employed on the ill-fated Tay Bridge across the Firth of Tay at Dundee. Tom had two younger sisters, Mary and Annie.

Tom attended the Infant's and Girls' School on High Hill, now the St Herbert's Social Centre, and then went on to Crosthwaite Old School, then an elementary school for boys aged 7 to 14 years. The building was on the site of an ancient Free Grammar School, probably founded before Elizabethan times. Some of his schoolfellows left the Old School at eleven years to attend Keswick School, but Tom remained there until he left to start work.

Tom's attachment to the Old School lasted through his lifetime. He eventually became a school manager and the correspondent to the managers and wrote the definitive history of the School, 'The History and Chronicles of Crosthwaite Old School', illustrated with his own drawings. Tom was also a manager of the Crosthwaite Girls' School on High Hill, a governor of Lairthwaite Secondary Modern School when it opened in 1952 and a trustee of the Keswick School of Industrial Arts, a venture begun by his vicar, Canon H. D. Rawnsley in 1884.

Tom was fortunate in having Mr Henry Swinburn as his headmaster at

Crosthwaite Old School. Prior to Henry Swinburn's appointment the school had been in dire straits. To quote George Bott, absenteeism was rife, standards were low and staff were often poorly qualified. Children were kept off school to run errands, to help on the farm or assist with visitors. Bad weather all too often provided an excuse for non-attendance. Many parents showed little interest in the welfare of their children and the school itself was cold and uninviting - on 23rd January 1879 the Log Book records that 'scholars had no writing on account of ink being frozen in inkwells'.

It was into this situation of apathy and inefficiency that Henry Swinburn was appointed in 1891. A new era began. Henry Swinburn was a trained teacher and served as headmaster at Crosthwaite for the next thirty-five years, a highly regarded and active member of the community, becoming chairman of the Keswick Urban Council amongst other offices held in the community.

Within a year, the quality of education had improved. Swinburn's discipline was severe and his expectations were high. He soon established Crosthwaite's reputation as a well-equipped school with, it was claimed, the best attainments in the county. He set high standards and pioneered innovations such as gardening, woodwork, weather recording and local studies.

The presence of the indefatigable Canon Rawnsley as vicar also benefited the school ethos. With those two people in charge, H. D. Rawnsley as chairman of the managers and Henry Swinburn as headmaster, Tom's future work in the community was nurtured. Indeed, when the then vicar, Canon Marshall, spoke at Tom's funeral he said that he 'had inherited the mantle of Rawnsley', which was praise indeed.

Tom's father was in business as a grocer in the building which is now occupied by the Edinburgh Woollen Mill, next to the Post Office. When Tom left school he worked as a baker for his father in the rear of the premises and continued working there until he took over the business when his father retired in 1921. Tom worked alongside his two sisters in the family business. Anne worked 'front of house' whilst Mary, who had been sent to London to learn the craft, was the confectioner. In later years and until the outbreak of the second world war Mary, her husband Clem and son John lived on the premises.

The influence of the headmaster of Crosthwaite Old School was all -

The former Waverley Hotel & Cafe

pervading. On one occasion Tom had placed an advertising board outside the Waverley Hotel offering residential accommodation, with 'accommodation' mis-spelt. On the following day a stream of boys from the school called on Mr Wilson enquiring how to spell 'accommodation'.

But it was not all work for Tom. He recalled how he travelled on the Buttermere Round as a young man - the four shillings and sixpence fare took him on a four-horse carriage from the Lake Hotel over the Honister and Newlands passes - with the gentlemen being required to walk on the steepest parts. This was before the road was metalled, and when boys earned tips using wedges or 'slips' to prevent the carriages careering down the steep inclines.

By 1925 Tom had enlarged the premises and closed the grocery. The bakery and confectionary business flourished with the return of Mary from her London training and Tom reopened re-opened the premises as a private hotel - a temperance hotel, which he named 'The Waverley' after the Waverley novels of Sir Walter Scott. Tom remembered entertaining Beatrix Potter to lunch when she attended the Annual Tup (Ram) Fair on Town's Field - but as Mrs William Heelis of course. Being a temperance hotel with no alcoholic drinks served, the hotel was cheaper than others and attracted many cyclists at a time when cycling in the Lake District was becoming very popular. The CTC (Cyclists Touring Club) sign on the hotel frontage is now on the door of the cycle repair workshop of Ian Hindmarch at Braithwaite.

Tom Wilson and Staff of the Waverley Hotel and Café, circa 1925 (Tom's sister Mary is first left, sitting, and his sister Annie, the cashier, is standing extreme right)

The business prospered with a staff of twenty-one. Tom married a local girl, Elizabeth Hogarth ('Aunt Lizzie' to her nephews) - described as 'a good woman behind a good man'. Tom and Elizabeth had no children of their own, but Tom spent a great deal of time with his two nephews, John Rigg and Stephen Hogarth. Elizabeth survived Tom and died in 1969. She had worked for some time as an uncertificated teacher of infant children at the school on High Hill and took in guests, as many other Keswick housewives did, and still do.

Tom ran the business successfully until the outbreak of war in 1939, when individual evacuees, schools and other educational institutions looked to Keswick to provide safe accommodation for the war years and found a warm welcome awaiting. St Katharine's College from Liverpool, a teacher-training establishment, took over the Waverley Hotel. The college had a large number of students billeted in other parts of the town but used the hotel as a catering centre with Tom assisting with the baking and general running of the restaurant.

A prestigious girls' school arrived to take over the Keswick Hotel - Roedean School from Sussex. The girls quickly integrated themselves into the town's activities and Tom introduced several to bellringing at Crosthwaite Church, where they became part of the bellringing team. As

Crosthwaite Bellringers with Tom Wilson left at rear & three Roedean girls (with ties)

with other evacuees, living in Keswick was a revelation to these children from both urban and rural locations in the south and the north-east of England. Tom was often busy lecturing to the St Katharine's College students about the 'Helm Wind', which comes down Skiddaw's flanks, and explaining the use of the meteorological instruments at the rear of School House on High Hill.

When the college left Keswick at the end of the war - leaving several girls here who had married local men - Tom immersed himself in his voluntary activities once again. He had always been a member of Crosthwaite church, and was one of the bellringers for over fifty years. With other bellringers he earned a final resting place in the bell ringers' plot at the south end of the church, where he and Elizabeth are buried. He sang in the choir as a boy, was a churchwarden, a sidesman and a parochial church councillor.

The Lakes Pavilion was the place to be on a Saturday evening for dancing or for other events during the week. Kelly's Directory of 1897 advertised the Pavilion as 'charmingly situated, overlooking Fitz Park and

St Kentigern's Church (Denys Valentine)

the River Greta with splendid mountain scenery and a dining room capable of seating six hundred'. What the advertisement did not say was that the building was erected on the site of an old tanyard, and that the animal skins were washed in the Greta below!

During the world war two years the PUPs organised many events to raise funds to send 'comforts' to the local men serving abroad, including 'fags for the lads'. On one memorable occasion the Pavilion had been booked by the PUPs for a dance several months in advance. Fortuitously, the date coincided with VE Day. The Pavilion had never been as full before or since.

Tom was often at the Pavilion producing or taking part - or both - in a musical event, or with children's parties, whist drives and other social occasions. The Pavilion was also used as a cinema, for conferences and one-day sales and then as a discotheque and wine bar. Many famous artists appeared there, including the singer Paul Robeson. With entertainment in the town becoming generally more available and the advent of television, the Lakes Pavilion became less used and ended its life as a roller skating rink. It was finally demolished in 1987, to the regret of many townsfolk, and replaced by the Riverside Lodge apartments.

Tom was passionately interested in the history of the church on which he was an acknowledged authority. He wrote booklets on its history and that of the church windows - they are still available for sale - a booklet *Let's Go For a Walk*, a guide to Keswick and district and *All About Keswick, a guide with maps,*, written with the humour which all had come to expect from him. The advice to tourists included 'Don't go rock climbing alone, or badly shod. Your obituary notice may be interesting, though not for you'. For many years he enthralled visitors to the church with his 'Monday Night at Eight' tours. The donations made were in aid of the church and especially the repair and refurbishment of the church clock, which like the Moot Hall clock, had only one hand, showing the hours. Tom also 'rescued' the old banner of the 'Skiddaw Greys', the volunteer corps set up by Dr David Ross Lietch of Portinscale to help protect the country in the time of the Napoleonic wars, the then equivalent of the Home Guard of the second world war. The restored banner is displayed in the church.

Tom was very active in promoting Keswick as a tourist resort and gave many amusing illustrated talks to a wide variety of organisations, including the Worker's Travel Association, the Holiday Fellowship and to most of the women's institutes in the north of the county. Tom illustrated his talks with his own colour slides. He always stressed the need to take care of the environment, to close gates and take home any litter. He was so popular with the ladies of the W I that on one occasion it was suggested that he become an honorary member!

The town's newspaper, The Keswick Reminder, prints regular weather reports from a voluntary meteorologist, Mr Ken Bond. The tradition of reporting the weather in the local press began with Tom Wilson, who kept records for thirty-four years. They were never merely concise reports, but enlivened by comments on his observations as a lover of nature. He took upon himself this duty from his former headmaster, from 1925 to 1956, as the official weather recorder for the Meteorological Service.

Tom's actual interest in weather recording dated back to his schooldays at Crosthwaite Old School, fostered by headmaster Henry Swinburn and Canon Rawnsley. To ensure that he was up-to-date with the technicalities of weather recording Tom once journeyed to Kew for a course of instruction on the subject.

Tom was proud of having not only Henry Swinburn's records but also those of Peter Crosthwaite, a noted Keswickian of his day. At the beginning of the second world war until early in 1946 Tom was the official meteorological recorder for the Keswick area. He was required to send weather reports on a daily basis, every hour from 4:50am to 7:50pm. He telephoned fifteen times each day, in code, weather reports to the Air Ministry, a total of over 28,000 messages. During the war there were several temporary airfields built on the Solway coast and in West Cumberland and the Air Ministry needed to know of weather conditions in the northern Lake District. In recognition of his services Tom was presented in 1956 with an inscribed barograph by the Director of the Meteorological Office, which is now in the proud possession of his nephew John. Only in 1959, when Tom was too ill to continue this service, did he retire from weather recording. Towards the end of this time he was helped in the recording duties by his sister Mary and nephew John.

Like many local people and visitors Derwentwater had a particular fascination for Tom. He became very interested in the varying levels of the water and recorded particularly low levels with the placing of slate plaques, with the date and often the initials of the then chairman of the then Urban District Council. He knew of Jonathan Otley, geologist and guide in Keswick, and followed his example in recording water levels. In 1955 Tom wrote a scholarly account in the *Keswick Reminder* of the life of Jonathan Otley, who lived and worked in a first floor room in King's Head Court, by the Moot Hall.

Tom thought that, of all his various activities, the happiest was that remarkable organisation which he founded with Harold Usher in 1927. It was known as the PUPs - the Pushing Young People's Society. Tom became known as 't' PUP Chap', which is how he signed his dialect articles in the *Keswick Reminder*. He became the first President of the Society. The PUP's Annuals, of which five were published each Christmas from 1931 to 1935, were a festive season delight for Keswickians. The booklets were sold for 'a bob', five pence in today's coinage, to help in the society's fund-raising. Tom Wilson was the editor (who else?) who used his skills as a cartoonist to enhance each volume. The booklets were a veritable mine of information on the history of Keswick and neighbourhood and Keswick matters and personalities - written with the wry humour that townsfolk expected from the editor and contained little nuggets of

Keswick history, for instance the names of the first men to own a motor car in the town and the make of the vehicles.

Tom's descriptions of local personalities pulled no punches, but were written in such a way that they caused no harm, and he was self-deprecating when writing of himself. The 'victims' quite enjoyed the notoriety! How could they be offended? Their names had appeared in the 'Annual'!

The 1931 edition - the first - contains a well-crafted poem in dialect recounting 'T' Christenin' of Liza Jane', the new fire engine for the town, and begins:

We've gitten a brand new ingin, aw brass an' pentid red,
It's gaen ta put awt' fires oot, like t' auld en thet we hed,
This en gah's be t'sell on 't, ivery things aw breet,
It'll git ta fire and hev it oot, afore its weel aleet.

The Council decided that the new fire engine was to be christened with an outing to include the councillors and officials on board. The journey started well, but the driver was not in full control of the 'ingin', causing it to overturn and the passengers to be spilled on to the road.

Eventually all was put right and the fire engine was christened 'Liza Jane', 'chrissened when nobbut a bairn, she behaved like a bairn seah they tellt ma, but when she's older she'll larn'.

Rock climbing has a long history in the Keswick area. In the Annuals Tom regularly reported on and cartooned the climbing exploits of the 'Crimson Ramblers', all PUPs members. In one edition Tom drew the group climbing a cliff, gathering mushrooms as they went. Hanging on the rope were Fred Phillipson, Dick Forsyth, Brian Mayton, Charlie Bone, Edgar Rushfirth, Joe Peascod, Tom Pape - and at the top of the cliff, hauling them all skywards, was Ralph Mayson of photographic postcard fame.

The PUPs, and perhaps particularly their president and editor, thoroughly enjoyed every minute of the various fund-raising activities, always conducted with humour and friendliness. All the activities were undertaken with a deep pride and love for their native town. As their Annuals always arrived shortly before Christmas, there was always the greeting 'Merry Kursmass ivverybody, noo pay yer shillings!'

The societies and clubs that Tom belonged to were legion. These included the Freemasons, the Rotary Club of Keswick, of which he became an honorary member, the Fitz Park Trustees, the Keswick Beekeepers Association, the Keswick Agricultural Society, the Trustees of the Keswick Museum and Art Gallery, the Cumberland and Westmorland Antiquarian and Archaeological Society and the local Committee of the Friends of the Lake District. He was also very proud of the carnations he grew in his heated greenhouse on High Hill.

One can see the influence his vicar, Canon Rawnsley, had on Tom's interests. He was a member of the local committee of the National Trust, of which Canon Rawnsley was a co-founder, and the Cumberland Dialect Society (now the Lakeland Dialect Society), the Keswick Publicity Association, the Amateur Operatic and Dramatic Society (of which he was a producer for twelve years), the Keswick Male Voice Choir, the Keswick Choral Society, the Christy Minstrels, giving concerts around the countryside before the First World War, the British Legion and many more. He never became a Town Councillor, although many wished him to, preferring to work for his town in his own way. He was truly the 'Mr Keswick' of his day.

When Tom died in 1961 many individuals and organisations wrote and spoke of their appreciation of the work he had done for the community. The then editor of the Keswick Reminder wrote 'There is a very large gap in the precincts of High Hill, a gap which has sent its repercussions into the ancient parish of Crosthwaite, and many other surrounding parishes in addition, a gap that will cause a void in the hearts of a great many souls. Tom's demise, though it had been anticipated, has rent the hearts of many, causing real grief to a host of his affectionate admirers. He was so beloved by all, and deservedly so, because of his uprightness of example and the sincerity of his thoughts'.

At his funeral service, Canon Harold Marshall spoke of Tom's life with humour. 'Tom was part of the Keswick scenery, and the very landscape will seem different now he had gone. He knew more about the Church and all connected with it than any other living person, for he donned the mantle Canon Rawnsley laid down. He served the Church in every capacity except that of Vicar - but he endeavoured to keep that gentleman on the straight and narrow path!'

Tom would have been proud of that accolade. There cannot have been any Keswickian before or since who cared so much for his native town and the people who lived there.

Further reading:
Colonel H C Wylly: *The Border Regiment in the First World War,* 1924
George Bott: *Keswick - The Story of a Lake District Town,* 1994
Tom Wilson: *The History and Chronicles of Crosthwaite Old School,* 1949 (and other publications)

Thanks for assistance to:
Sally Dixon, Ronnie Green, Robert Grisdale, Elsie Hindmoor, Stephen Hogarth, Liz Martland, John Rigg, Jean Taylor and Jeff Taylor.
Special thanks to Stuart Eastwood, Museum Curator, the Regimental Museum of the Border Regiment and the King's Own Royal Border Regiment at The Castle, Carlisle.

RAY 'MAC' McHAFFIE (1936 - 2005)
Rock and ice climber and footpath builder

Tony Greenbank

Blinded in one eye as a youth by a teddy boy with an axe, Raymond McHaffie, who died just before Christmas 2005 aged 69, rarely looked back with the remaining good one. It was as well that when he left the Carlisle timber yard where he worked for 14 years, prior to his arrival in Keswick in the early 1950s, he was the only employee still to have all his fingers and all his toes intact. He was in charge of cleaning the teeth on the big saw. One raw winter morning his hands froze so fast to the cold metal his workmates could only free them by pouring kettles of hot water over them.

Mac - as he was known - was indomitable. Once he cut into his thigh with a chainsaw while at work on logs. As blood poured out of the wound, and the Irish foreman fainted, he was heard to say: 'Another good pair of jeans ruined'. He walked to the office, which was some distance away, and somehow got to hospital. Shortly afterwards he inadvertently tore the stitches out while soloing Monolith Crack on Shepherd's Crag in Borrowdale.

His muscular sturdy stature, stoic disposition and a total disregard for danger, allied with those prehensile extremities, brought him a tally of 250 rock climbs recorded in the Fell and Rock Climbing Club's Borrowdale guidebook. A famous occasion was when he climbed an exciting route climb for television in boxing gloves and roller skates. Little Chamonix was the climb chosen for this stunt, for a bet. Would Bentley Beetham have turned in his grave? Smiled indulgently, more like. For Mac was the worthy successor of this pioneer, veteran of an Everest expedition, whose earlier pioneering efforts - even to gardening cracks with a teaspoon - helped to popularise Borrowdale crags. ('Gardening' is the rock climber's term for removing vegetation from crevices to 'improve' a climb - a practice perhaps frowned up by environmentalists).

How well he filled this role, putting up classic ascents like The Niche (with Adrian Liddell), The Coffin, Savage Messiah and, thirty years later, the ever-popular classic Lakeland Cragsman. It was a regular sight to find him studiously licking a stub of pencil as he entered details of this or that death-defying climb he had just created in the battered ledger that served as a 'new routes book' in the Woolpack pub where Keswick 'crag rats' met.

Mac discovered not only individual routes, but whole 'new' crags too. His was the first line (Mercedes) on Car Park Buttress, also in Borrowdale, an event which led to him being warned off by other climbers, but conveyed to him second hand. He did not scare easily. During the fracas in Carlisle that cost him an eye he was not blameless. Leader himself of a gang (in yellow suit with velvet collar, pink suede shoes and DA - duck's arse - haircut), he was only intent on causing chaos in the pubs and dance halls of 1950s Carlisle.

His parents separated while he was young, and Mac was brought up by his grandparents in Carlisle. But it was in the toughest part of the city. Then a friend, Joe Bernie, suggested they visit the Lakes on the weekly fell walker's bus. During the following year the two teenagers became regular 'bussers', where Mac's witty utterances and monologues concerning the climbs done that day from the back seat, all delivered with a particularly penetrating voice, enlivened the passengers. Such was his derring-do on the crags, he was given three months to live by members of the Carlisle Mountaineering Club.

One Sunday Mac arrived hurt. He had cut a foot on broken glass when leaping from a raft on to a riverbed. Hobbling painfully and unable to keep up with the others, he still reached Kern Knotts despite the eight fresh sutures underfoot. Seeing The Crack and The Chimney, he soloed both - one foot in a bendy boot, the other in a carpet slipper. No one on the bus believed him, so the following week he returned with his doubting audience and repeated the climbs.

Then Mac moved on along the airy climber's track high across the fell side to cross Great Hellgate Screes, overlooked by the awesome sight of Tophet Wall, Great Gable. Around the corner is Napes Needle, and the sight of the famous obelisk stark against the sky drew him like a magnet. Without knowing what was involved he began to climb. On the crux move, he was struggling to 'mantelshelf' when a monk appeared, habit tucked up into his rope-end waist-tie. A second monk followed, and Mac was invited to share their rope. On top he heard himself say, 'This is' - and he swore - 'dangerous.' The leader replied 'I think it is time you went down.'

During 1952 Mac began hitching to Keswick after timber yard work on Saturday mornings. He stayed bed and breakfast for 2/6d a night with an elderly lady. The Golden Lion was the pub; the Pavilion, the dancehall and ring. The stars: Don Whillans, Pete Greenwood, Paul Ross. It was a hard school and the young tearaway learned gradually, broadening his horizons beyond the area. Forever associated with Borrowdale, he climbed the hardest routes of his heyday on the fiercest British crags, be it The Right Unconquerable on Stanage in Derbyshire or Kilnsey Crag Overhang in Wharfedale (with pegs); Cenotaph Corner above Llanberis Pass or Centurion on Ben Nevis.

That early upbringing on the Raffles estate in Carlisle left its mark. Mac always said he was lucky he found climbing. Otherwise, like most of his peers of that time, he would have ended up in prison. Until he found escape via the fell walker's bus, his experience of the great outdoors had been playing nine-card brag in a field by the estate. As always he enlivened the scene, later founding the Raffles Alpine Club - a direct opposite of the august body of that name which is based in London.

Mac had a trial for Carlisle United Football Cub as goalkeeper, being pipped to the post (literally) by Allan Ross who was to become a crowd favourite through the years. Once he won a drinking competition versus Adrian Liddell in the Friars Tavern, Carlisle. He arrived first and ordered a pint. No sooner had he taken a swallow than his 'adversary' arrived. 'How many pints have you had?' asked a distraught Ado, apologetic for being late and keen to make amends. 'Four,' replied McHaffie. The young Liddell could not order four pints quickly enough, swallow them in virtually one go and continue the contest on a one-for-one basis - only to succumb.

Crag climbs succumbed to Mac's persistence, though not without a battle. On The Chasm on Glencoe's Buchaille Etive Mor in winter, companion Les Kendall had never seen Mac so spent. 'Pull, Les, pull!' Mac gasped arriving at the stance after ice pitch. Then Les saw why. The flap of his Alpine rucksac had come adrift. The Devil's Cauldron waterspout had filled his bag so full of water it weighed 70lbs at least. After Les poured the water out Mac made an instant recovery. 'It had me worried,' he admitted. 'I thought my so-and-so arms had gone!'

By contrast his wit was dry, and never deserted him. A university lecturer once corrected him when, in his inimitable and rather penetrating voice, Mac had said a rock face had only 'minnit' holds. Surely you mean 'minute'?' said the lecturer. 'No, I mean 'minnit',' said McHaffie. 'You can only stand on 'em a minnit before your legs start shekking.'

Another time Mac was avalanched 1,000 feet on Great End and catapulted over a crag before being buried alive among the avalanche debris. He forced his way out despite having difficulty in breathing and a horrible pain in his chest. Realising he had dropped his brand-new Charlet-Moser ice axe in the process, he climbed all the way back up to the top to retrieve it. Next day the doctor told him he had broken two ribs.

In the Alps Mac's ascents included the South Face of the Marmolata and Vajolet Towers with no mentor other than the spirit of Hermann Buhl (and pages torn from Buhl's 'Nanga Parbat Pilgrimage'). Mac had hoped to make the first British ascent of the North Wall of the Eiger with Brian Nally, only his grandmother died, meaning Nally - short of a climbing partner - subsequently teamed up with Barry Brewster who was killed on the second icefield. Nally was rescued by Don Whillans and Chris Bonington who were making their own attempt.

Known for his pithy utterances, which earned him the sobriquet the 'Jaws of Borrowdale' (a route on Recastle Crag is called White Noise because of his running commentary during the first ascent), his climbing achievements won Mac wholehearted respect. This was mirrored in the acclamation he also received for the footpath and conservation work he achieved with his National Trust footpath repair gang.

For 21 years he and his team of trailblazers worked in all weathers on the highest Lake District slopes rebuilding ancient footpaths by the score. Today they are trodden by hundreds of thousands of fell walkers each year. As the longest serving footpath builder in the UK, he was on familiar terms with the going getting tough. There were times when 60mph winds tore the shovels out of the hands of his gang, sending them flying through the air so that other members of the team had to leap out of the way. One spade scored a direct hit on another member of the gang who was 10 yards distant at the time.

Once Mac dropped a boulder the weight of a bag of cement on his calf muscles as he slipped, fell and twisted. He watched his leg turn black and blue from top to bottom. He estimated that he and his gang manoeuvred and lifted and manhandled some of the biggest slabs of rock since the creation of Stonehenge. Huge granite rocks yielded as Mac and his lads (and lasses) heaved them up out of the ground by the Turfor winch - like a capstan on a ship where the crew strain on the bars and the load is moved little by little an inch at a time by wire ropes and brute strength and know-how.

Today the traffic is even heavier on Sty Head as booted legions are drawn to the magnets of Great Gable and Scafell Pike, all treading the ways Mac paved with his Borrowdale Footpath Team - including stalwarts John Pearson, Kevin Tyson and Keith Wolstencroft - and any number of volunteers, many from the Prince's Trust. Some of his paths won awards, including European accolades. Mac lectured at the Royal Festival Hall in London on the intricacies of footpath building to members of the National Trust in their thousands.

A scientist calculated that he had helped construct over 100 miles of paved highway on the windswept heights during his years of footpath building on Lakeland mountains from Scafell to Thresthwaite Cove above Hartsop. He estimated that Mac had walked a distance equivalent to going to the moon and back in terms of travelling to and from work high on the Lakeland hills on foot - and in the process building mountain footpaths.

Day after day, week by week, through successive years, the National

Trust Land Rover dropped Mac and his gang off below one mountain pass or another. From there they have slogged for six or seven miles up the towering fell side beetling overhead - to the part of the footpath from which they left off the previous day - and then later made their weary way down before nightfall. For two weeks he camped on the summit of Scafell Pike, the highest mountain in England at 3206ft when he and John Garner and Andrew Warner demolished the vast summit cairn - 37 yards in circumference and 7ft tall - and rebuilt it in the interests of safety. The cairn had been on the point of collapse under the weight of people clambering over it to become 'the highest in the land'.

The original plan was for a Sea King helicopter to ferry the cairn-builders' supplies to the summit. But two RAF jets had crashed in Borrowdale the previous day and the dale was off-limits for military aircraft. The intrepid mountain men were obliged to walk from Seathwaite instead, carrying 70lbs each in sacks - equivalent to a sack of coal each. On arrival at the top they dumped their load, then returned to Seathwaite by 1pm. Refilling their sacks, they went back to the top, complete with tents, cookers, food, water - and some alcoholic refreshment.

Drystone walling was a Mac speciality. He said he learned the art from an old-timer called Matt Barnes of Thornthwaite, with whom he worked with when he first arrived to live in Keswick. It led to a number of jobs that offered welcome remuneration. One night there was a knock on the

Mac belaying.

door. It was the art director from Granada TV - on an errand from film director Ken Russell. 'Ken wants you to build him a man,' he said. Mac responded 'I'm not a surgeon.' 'No, a stone man,' was the reply. 'Twelve feet high. Two legs, two arms. With a top hat. And a view of Buttermere and Crummock Water between its legs.'

It was, Mac learned, for a film about Wordsworth and Coleridge called 'Clouds of Glory'. Wordsworth and his sister had built a stone man in their garden. Years later Wordsworth wrote in a poem that it was a monolithic man and Ken Russell wanted a real Mac-type monolithic man. Everyone marvelled at the result and agreed it was awesome, perhaps too much so. Mac said at the time, 'I suddenly realised it would be a magnet for kids clambering up it. The whole thing weighed tons. So I decided to knock it. I knocked away a leg under it, which wasn't easy. It crashed down with a hell of a noise.'

That evening the art director called round again, saying, 'Mac, your stone man's fallen down.' 'No it hasn't. I knocked it down.' 'Well, there's a camera case been accidentally left in view in one of shots. We're not sure whether we will able to use it. You'll have to rebuild it.' 'Well, I'm not going to.' Fortunately, he said they found a way round the problem and he was not pressed to do any more stone-man-building.

Sty Head Pass was his first footpath project in 1980, the popular track from Stockley Bridge at the head of Borrowdale over the hills to Wasdale. Like all the other paths he was to upgrade, it had been all but trampled to death. Travellers, pack trains and smugglers all walked this way. There was also the literary association with Hugh Walpole's 'Herries Chronicles'. Today the traffic between Stockley Bridge and the mountain-rescue stretcher box on the summit of Sty Head is even heavier. The footpath erosion, Mac remembered, at the top of the first steep section, past the well known 1,000ft. boulder, had been increased by the heavy rainfall of the area to produce six to eight foot deep ruts. In parts there were perhaps ten alternative footpaths over a 40-yard area. The National Trust decided one good path system was needed to erase this unsightly and dangerous erosion and prospected for an alternative line.

An old cobbled, or pitched, packhorse route was found hidden away among the bracken and gave the lead on the techniques to apply to the new path. The path was sometimes pitched on a new line and sometimes on the existing line, to link in with the old route which could have gone back two hundred years. As walkers at the time observed, some of the pitching bedded in so well after a period of around four months it was difficult to tell which was the two hundred year old section and which was Mac's.

Mac's paths were usually of the pitched variety he created on Sty Head, and built on a simple principle: dig a ditch 1ft deep and 4ft wide - the length of a shovel - and fill it with big rocks or 'cobbles', interlocking them together like the pieces of a jigsaw puzzle. Fill up the cracks with gravelly stones which bond everything together. Finally add soil on top - and sow grass seed along the verges.

The loftiest pitched path engineered by Mac and his team was to the summit of Scafell plateau at 3,000 feet via Fox's Tarn - the highest footpath in England. For eighteen months they laboured, walking the laborious but also idyllic seven miles to and from work every day and in all weathers. It grieved Mac that the path was allowed to deteriorate as the National Trust stopped the regular maintenance work needed. He and his team classed it as one of the greatest efforts ever in terms of building a mountain footpath. Mac always held it was tragic to see it collapsing away.

Mac reckoned that previously his team used to maintain it every three or four months. This was because it was so exposed that the elements soon wreaked havoc. 'We were taken off the job by the head warden,' he said at the time, 'and the maintenance work was handed over to the Wasdale footpath team. Since then little repair work has been done on what was a truly great footpath.'

The Corridor Route from the summit of Sty Head to the summit of Scafell Pike was another tour de force. A major footpath, and in better repair, it snakes for miles over lunar-like terrain, crossing the gorge of Piers Gill. Mac and his team also re-created the Breast Route up Great Gable from the Sty Head first-aid box. Then they constructed what is the longest traditional cobbled path - between Armboth and Watendlath. Linking Thirlmere and Borrowdale by the old Coffin Road, he said this was at the time the best recovered path of any in the Lake District - a feather in his balaclava, especially as previously it had been in disrepair.

And the toughest? 'Two spring to mind,' he said. 'One was the path up Tongue Gill through Rigg Head mines above Rosthwaite. The other was up Stanger Ghyll in Langstrath which was by far the most demanding path we have ever built.'

Mac ice-climbing

In the case of Tongue Ghyll, Mac and his gang had to dig through an old quarry spoil heap on a very steep hillside and with masses of loose stones. 'It was the exact opposite of a garden path,' he says, adding that the effect of the large slabs of slate that eventually went to make up the path is one of the most visually attractive byways he ever built.

'The Stanger Ghyll footpath was just plain desperate,' he says. 'It starts just above the campsite at Stonethwaite in Borrowdale and is popular with walkers heading for Bessyboot and Glaramara. We built it up solid, smooth polished rock slabs and it was extremely steep and precipitous. One day a solid steel bogey carrying several tons of stones got away, and it ended up a quarter of a mile downhill. Every time it bounced it knocked a wheel off. Luckily no one was in the way, and it missed all the trees in its path. It would have totally decimated anything in its tracks.'

During his two decades-plus working on the hill Mac had to put up with the occasional voice of dissent. A man who introduced himself as a doctor on the Breast Route of Great Gable threw a fit, shouting, 'I'm not walking down that path. It's a disgrace.' Mac watched him sit on his behind to negotiate the scree and replied 'That's up to you, sir. You'll find it much easier on the path.' The doctor was not the only one to offer comment. Hikers watching his gang labour away on the steep fell side might say, 'You'll be putting escalators in next'. And Mac would retort, 'If you pay for them, sir, I'll be glad to put them in.'

To see him at work was to see patience personified. To help ease the burden of the great rocks he manhandled with apparent ease he wore a leather weightlifter's belt. For food, he never ate through the day, only at suppertime. A flask of tea was his only sustenance on the hill and he always worked on through the mid-day break while his gang ate their 'bait', or he went cragging on the nearest cliff, delighting in the Fox's Tarn path because it was so close to the electrifying barrel-shaped East Buttress of Scafell.

When Mac retired in 1999 he turned his attention to cycling around Derwentwater, always with a pit stop at his beloved Shepherds Caff and a crack with mates like 'Yorkie', Sid and Aileen Clark and Colin Downer and so many more, including any member of Carlisle Mountaineering Club, and farmer Martin Weir (who could be making the scones and giving as good as he got). With his wife Margaret's help Mac made the garden of their Keswick home a veritable miniature National Park.

Painting in oils and watercolours also captivated him; many were the crag shots and landscapes he recreated as osteo-arthritis began to affect a hip in his retirement years and restrict his activities. And still he kept cragging, the one pastime he could never let go. Although he did eventually acquire a hip replacement, he was still to be seen on the crags in the months preceding the operation. He would never give in to adversity. Even the fact he suffered from Parkinson's disease did not stop him attempting to live as full a life as possible - as he always had succeeded in doing since he was that boy on the fell walker's bus.

Books Published by Bookcase

All books are available from the publisher at 19 Castle Street, Carlisle, CA3 8SY, (01228 544560) or from www.bookscumbria.com.

Keswick: The Story of a Lake District Town. George Bott. £15
This elegant history tells the story of Keswick from the time of Castlerigg Stone Circle to the present day. Keswick has an importance far beyond its size. German miners came in Elizabethan times, the pencil was discovered here, it was a key centre of the Romantic revolution and later the town became famous for the Keswick Convention.

The Story of the Newlands Valley. Susan Grant. £12
Susan Grant's family have lived in the Newlands Valley near Keswick for over 350 years. Her detailed history draws on old records and extensive personal knowledge to paint a picture of a unique isolated community.

The Loving Eye and Skilful Hand: The Keswick School of Industrial Arts. Ian Bruce. £15.00
This is the first detailed study of the Keswick School. Founded by the Rawnsleys, the school became one of the most important centres of the Arts and Crafts movement. The book hsould be of great interest to historians and colectors.

A Canny History of Carlisle. Jim Eldridge. £7.99
Caught on the cusp between England and Scotland, Carlisle has a better story to tell than most cities. Our Canny Historian, Jim Eldridge,creator of Radio 4's King Street Junior, is just the chap to tell the tale of the Great Border City - from the days of the Celts and the Romans right up to the floods and the football team.

Carlisle to Canada: A Family Chronicle. Cathy Smith £8.99
Cathy Smith discovered a bundle of old letters in her grandmother's house in Melbourne Road, Carlisle. They told of an Edwardian romance and of emigaration to Canada and the parallel lives two families led in Carlisle and on a prairie farm.

The Wigton Memorial Fountain Solway History Society £10
In 2004 Solway History Society restored the George Moore Memorial Fountain which stands in the centre of Wigton. This book tells the story of the fountain and of George Moore who built it as a memorial to his wife, Eliza. There is a detailed photographic record of the Fountain itself and a pictorial record of the Fountain through the years.

**Strong Lad Wanted For Strong Lass: Growing Up In Carlisle
Hunter Davies £8.99**
Hunter Davies tells the story of his early years in Carlisle before and after the Second World War. Hunter is one of the country's best known writers and journalists, author of over 30 books.
Hurry, Hurry, While Stocks Last. Hunter Davies.   £7.95
A sideways look at the economic, social and shopping history of Cumbria as seen through local advertisements 1850-1940. Hunter Davies traces the changes in Cumbrian life, in attitudes and activities, trends and fashions.
The Ghosts of Cumbria. Laurie Kemp.   £6.99
Laurie Kemp has ventured fearlessly among the lakes and fells to uncover the stories of the uneasy spirits that lurk in dark and eerie houses.
A New Illustrated History of Wigton   John Higham   £11.50
A detailed, well-researched history spanning nearly two thousand years of this small market town.
Cumberland and Westmorland Wrestling.   Roger Robson   £8.95
A modern history of Cumberland and Westmorland wrestling.
Border Television: A History. Mary Scott Parker.   £7.95
A collection of personal memories from the local broadcasters who have been involved in the television station over the years.
A Border Naturalist: The Birds & Wildlife of the Bewcastle Fells & the Gilsland Moors, 1930 - 1966   Ritson Graham   £10.00
A beautifully written study of the rich and varied wildlife in one of the last unspoilt areas of the country.
The Antique County Maps of Cumberland   John Higham.   £11.99
The lavishly illustrated story of the printed maps of Cumberland.
The Anatomy of the Helm Wind. David Uttley.   £9.95
A unique study which examines the only named wind in Britain.
Beatys Illustrated Guide to Carlisle £2.95
A facsimile reprint of the original guide from 1905, first designed to show the Edwardian tourist the finer sights of the flourishing Border city.
The Changing Face of Brampton. Iain Parsons.   £11.50
Over 150 rare photos and a detailed, informative text display the author's affection for this old cumbrian town.
Provincial Pleasures.   Norman Nicholson.   £7.00
A classic account of small town life fifty or more years ago by one of Cumbria's finest writers and poets.

History of Penrith. Ewanian (William Furness)   £7.50
A facsimile reprint of the original edition of 1894, giving a thorough history of Penrith and district up to the end of the nineteenth century.

The Black Angel. Colin Bardgett.   £8.95
A valuable military record. The author has assembled diaries and letters written by men of the Penrith Volunteer Company who went to fight in the Boer War.

Silloth. Mary Scott-Parker.   £8.95
A nostalgic history of this charming Victorian seaside town.

The History of Wigton. Thomas W. Carrick.   £8.95
A facsimile reprint of Carrick's famous work.

Cockermouth Mechanics' Band.   Geoff Hunter.   £7.99
A history of the oldest band in Cumberland, richly illustrated throughout.

A Year At Ambleside: Harriet Martineau At Ambleside   Harriet Martineau; Barbara Todd   £10.00
Includes the first UK publication of A Year at Ambleside *by the great Victorian thinker and feminist Harriet Martineau.*

Gretna's Secret War. Gordon L. Routledge.   £7.95
In 1915 the greatest munitions factory on Earth was built at Gretna.

Carlisle Cathedral History.   David W.V. Weston   £14.95
The first detailed account of how the Cathedral buildings have developed and changed over the centuries. The closely illustrated text provides a comprehensive record of a wonderful building.

Longtown. Gordon L. Routledge.   £11.95
Longtown, the last town in England, was an important crossing point on the River Esk on the border between Scotland and England. This scrapbook of the town, its history and people is an affectionate celebration of a unique place

Carlisle and its Villages. Vincent White.   £11.95
An attractive collection of pen and ink drawings of old buildings in and around Carlisle. Vincent White began making these pictures as he saw familiar sights being demolished before his eyes.

Murder in Cumbria. Ian Ashbridge.   £8.95
Ian Ashbridge researches the murders that have been committed in the beautiful county of Cumbria in the twentieth century.